Fancy That!
Antique Costumes and Accessories, 1850–1925

Florence Theriault

Gold Horse Publishing

© 2004 Theriault's Gold Horse Publishing. All rights reserved.
No part of this book may be reproduced or utilized in any form or by any means, electronic or mechanical, including photocopying, recording, or by any information retrieval system, without permission, in writing, from the author or the publisher.

To order additional copies contact:
Dollmasters
PO Box 2319
Annapolis, MD 21404
Tel. 800-966-3655, Fax 410-571-9605
www.dollmasters.com

Design by Deborah VanDereedt
Photography by Chris Brady and Colby Kuschatka

This book is based upon a collection of antique costumes and accessories auctioned by Theriault's of Annapolis, Maryland.

$39
ISBN: 1-931503-21-4
Printed in Hong Kong

Table of Contents

CHAPTER I:
Early Costumes, 1850–1865 4

CHAPTER II:
Fashion Doll Gowns, 1860–1875 20

CHAPTER III:
Bebe Dresses, 1875–1885 49

CHAPTER IV:
Sailor Dresses 96

CHAPTER V:
Jackets, Coats and Outerwear 106

CHAPTER VI:
Cotton Dresses, 1880–1930 118

Chapter I:
Early Costumes, 1850–1865

Engraving on box lid of child's sewing machine, #289.

1. Silk Plaid Day Dress for Elongated Slim-Bodied Doll
Soft silk in brown and bronze plaid features a very high waist with constructed waistband that is virtually hidden at the flat front of the gown, but strongly featured at the back with cartridge gathers above and below. There are pleats at the front bodice top that give shape to the dress but are covered by the capelet collar that extends nearly to the waistband. The sleeves are elongated and tied with silk ribbons, the gown is lined, and there is patterned silk ribbon edging down the front opening, sleeve bands and collar edging. To fit doll about 28". 3" shoulder width. $400/500   650

2. Transfer Print Cotton Sateen Costume
Of silk-like cotton sateen in rich transfer pattern of brown, red and blue, the costume comprises blouse with flower-patterned back and striped bodice, tightly fitted sleeves with some fullness at the shoulders, along with matching long skirt having set-in waist, box pleats at the front, cartridge pleating at the back. Along with matching petticoat and pantalets, and on old muslin body form. To fit slim-bodied doll about 17". 3 1/2" shoulder width. 6" waist. $200/300

3. Blue Velvet Slippers with Upturned Toes
Of lustrous midnight blue velvet shaped with upturned toes, velvet soles with leather cording, red leather cording around the upper edges, patterned canvas lining. 3 1/4"l. $100/200

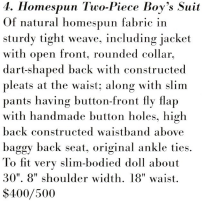

4. Homespun Two-Piece Boy's Suit
Of natural homespun fabric in sturdy tight weave, including jacket with open front, rounded collar, dart-shaped back with constructed pleats at the waist; along with slim pants having button-front fly flap with handmade button holes, high back constructed waistband above baggy back seat, original ankle ties. To fit very slim-bodied doll about 30". 8" shoulder width. 18" waist. $400/500

5. Brown Cotton Indigo Print Dress
Of two cotton patterns, in rich printed patterns of rust, brown and white, the floor-length dress is loosely fitted with flared sides, rounded neckline, coat sleeves, ten front buttons and handmade buttonholes. The entire front opening and cuffs are edged with a wide band of contrasting patterned fabric, and there are two wide bands of this border fabric at the hemline. To fit doll about 28". 7" shoulder width. $300/400

6. Blue/Brown Cotton Dress with Blue Embroidered Apron
Of intricate plaid in cream, blue and brown, the cotton dress features rounded neckline with self-cording, full length flat front with pearl button closure at the throat, full back bodice formed by gathers above the set-in waistband, cartridge pleating at the back to form generous gathers, self-cording at shoulders,

very full modified-gigot sleeves with pleats at the shoulders and constructed cuffs. Along with blue apron decorated with overcast embroidery at scallop-edged hem and white featherstitch trim. To fit doll about 16". 4" shoulder width. 7" waist. $400/500

7. Brown Calico Print Dress with Gigot Sleeves
Of brown cotton print with low rounded neckline, slightly dropped shoulders, fitted bodice, set-in waistband, full cartridge pleated skirt, gigot sleeves that achieve their shape from cartridge pleating at the shoulders, buttoned cuffs. To fit doll about 12". 3 1/2" shoulder width. 8" waist. $100/200

8. Petite Blue Patterned Cotton Dress
Of white crisp cotton with overall abstract pattern of blue leaves, the dress features a rounded neckline, dropped shoulders, scalloped sleeve bands, full bodice with gathers above the set-in waist, generously gathered skirt, hook-and-eye closure at waist, drawstring at back of neckline. To fit doll about 9". 2" shoulder width. 4" waist. $200/250

9. Blue and White Cotton Dress
Of crisp blue cotton in printed latticework design, the dress features full gathered bodice with shirring at the front and back waist, rounded neckline with self-cording, dropped shoulders, short sleeves over full length long sleeves with button-and-loop wrist closure, very full skirt with cartridge pleats all around. To fit doll about 24". 7" shoulder width. 12" waist. $300/400

10. Red Plaid Dress with Gigot Sleeves, and Linen Apron
Of red and blue homespun plaid, the dress features fitted bodice with front closure, shaped collar, set-in waistband above cartridge pleated skirt, exaggerated gigot sleeves with very full gathering at shoulders, constructed cuffs. Along with linen apron with embroidered edging, two embroidered pockets. To fit doll about 18". 4 1/2" shoulder width. 8" waist. $600/800

11. Brown Cotton Print Dress
Of rich cotton print in shades of grey, brown and russet, the dress features slim bodice with dart shaping that curves in a matching arc with the self-corded dropped shoulders, V-shaped neckline that corresponds to the V-shaped waist defined by self-cording, long slim-fitting sleeves, full skirt that is box-pleated at the front, with cartridge pleats at the back, hook-and-eye closure. To fit doll about 15". 4" shoulder width. 8" waist. $300/400

12. Cobbler's Leather and Wooden Shoes
Of very thick handcut and stitched leather, the shoe is designed to clasp over the top of the foot, with slightly upturned toes, tongue, and thick wooden soles with defined heels edged by a border of brass studs. 5 1/2"l. $100/200

13. Cotton Print Dress with Shirring at Waist
Of finely woven cream cotton with lavender printed flowers, the gown features a rounded neckline with self-cording, very full bodice shaped from a 1" panel of shirring just above the set-in waistband, slightly dropped shoulders with shirring detail, elbow-length trumpet sleeves with scalloped-edge, very full gathered skirt, pearl button-and-loop back closures, hook-and-eye at waist. To fit doll about 16". 4" shoulder width. 8" waist. $200/300

14. Petite White Flower-Sprigged Dress with Blue Apron
Of white crisply starched cotton printed with delicate blue flower sprigs, the dress features a rounded neckline edged with delicate lace, long sleeves with set-in cuffs with buttons and buttonholes, set-in waistband above a full gathered skirt, button-and-loop closure. Along with blue chambray apron with embroidered navy blue edging, two pockets with embroidery, set-in waistband. To fit doll about 12". 2" shoulder width. 5" waist. $400/500

15. Cotton Print Dress with Bonnet, Basket and Sabots
Cream cotton dress with tiniest abstract pattern of rose-colored flowers, the dress features an intricately shaped bodice with very fine shirring at the waist, gathered bodice, rounded neckline, dropped shoulders, unusual short sleeves with handmade lace borders over long sleeves with matching borders, cartridge pleated skirt. Included is green silk quilted bonnet with rose lining, woven workbasket with lid in shades of green and rose, and wooden sabots with carved decorations. To fit doll about 18". 4 1/2" shoulder width. 9" waist. $500/700

16. Navy Blue/Cream Shadowpane Checkered Dress
Of navy blue/cream shadowpane print, the rounded neck dress with fitted bodice has slightly dropped shoulders, trumpet sleeves gathered at the shoulders, set-in waist with V-shape at center waist, full skirt formed from double pleats all around, hook-and-eye closure, trimmed at bodice, cuffs and hem with black/brown interwoven braid. To fit doll about 17". 4" shoulder width. 8" waist. $200/250

17. Cotton Plaid Dress with Silk Ribbons
Of intricately woven brown, cream and red plaid with rounded neckline, self-cording at neckline and shoulders, fitted bodice with set-in darts at back, set-in waist, 3/4 sleeves with pagoda shaped sleeves, flat-front very full skirt with pleats forming into box pleats at the back of the gown, hook-and-eye closure. The dress is decorated with borders of pleated silk plaid with fringed edging. To fit doll about 17". 4" shoulder width. 7" waist. $300/400

18. Brown Silk/Linen Dress with Handmade Black Rick-Rack
Of textured silk/linen in richly mottled brown shade, the dress features a low square-cut neckline, fitted bodice, dropped shoulders, short trumpet sleeves, set-in waistband, flat-front, full skirt formed by box pleats at the sides and gathers at the back, hook-and-eye closure, detachable sash. The dress is trimmed with double rows of handmade black rick-rack at the bodice, sleeves and hem, and one row on the sash. To fit doll about 16". 4" shoulders. 8" waist. $200/300

19. Brown/Gold Striped Silk/Linen Dress with Cape
Of a fine silk/linen fabric with an unusual design of brown stripes and red pencil stripes on gold background, the dress features a rounded neckline, front closure bodice with hook-and-eye at the set-in waistband, bodice fullness achieved by cartridge pleats above the waistband and at the shoulders, box pleats at the front full skirt, and cartridge pleats at the back. The dress has very full lantern sleeves with elaborately constructed pleats at the shoulders, constructed sleeve bands with button-and-loop closure. There is a bronze silk edging at the hem and neckline, and a bronze silk waist tie. Along with matching cape with bronze silk edging and ties. To fit doll about 16". 4" shoulder width. 8" waist. $400/500

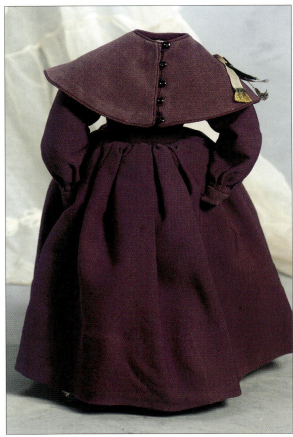

20. Brown Handweave Linen Dress
Of coarsely textured handwoven brown linen, the dress features a rounded V-shaped neckline with dart shaping at front, side-front overlapping closure, constructed waist above a full skirt with neatly shaped double box pleats at front and gathers at the back, short fitted sleeves with faux cuffs. To fit doll about 22". 6" shoulder width. 12" waist. $300/400

21. Lilac Woolen Gown with Cape
Of rich lilac-colored wool, the gown features a dart-shaped fitted bodice with self-cording at rounded neckline, set-in wide waistband, slightly dropped shoulders with cording, very full long sleeves with set-in cuffs, full gathered skirt. Along with matching short capelet with brown cotton sateen lining, five black buttons and loops, bows and streamers of lavender, green and ivory. To fit doll about 15". 3" shoulder width. 7" waist. $200/300

22. Brown Leather Lacing Boots with Heels
Of soft brown leather with black decorative stitching and white cotton lining, the boots feature curved shape at top edging, five pairs of brass-edged lacing grommets, thick leather soles with added wooden heels. The workmanship is superb yet the size of the shoes indicate its original production as doll shoe. 3"l. $400/500

23. Canvas and Leather Ankle Boots
Of hand-woven soft canvas with leather uppers and soft leather soles, the ankle boots have soft leather soles and four pairs of hand-stitched lacing holes, cord laces. 3"l. $200/300

24. Silver Metallic-Fabric Gown with Metallic Braid
Of superb early silver metallic fabric that is interwoven or embroidered with delicately colored flowers, the gown features a low square-cut bodice, dropped shoulders, fitted bodice, elbow-length trumpet sleeves with double row of lace edging, set-in waistband, full skirt formed from all around pleats. The gown is trimmed with borders of metallic lace. The dress is fully lined. To fit doll about 18". 6" shoulder width. 14" waist. $500/700   *725*

25. Sheer White Muslin Gown with Elaborate Bodice
Of sheer white finely woven muslin the gown features lace-edged rounded neckline above a bodice constructed of alternate horizontal bands of shirring and embroidery, short sleeves with cording at the armholes and embroidery and lace at the sleeve ends, constructed waist with cording trim, very full gathered skirt with seven wide horizontal tucks, drawstring closures at waist and back neckline. To fit doll about 17". 4 1/2" shoulders. 12" adjustable waist. $400/600

26. White and Cream Voile Dress
Of delicate voile with cream blouse attached to white skirt, the dress features a fitted bodice with shirring at the waist, narrow tucks at the shaped neck, Juliette-style long sleeves with very narrow tucks all around the lower arms, four buttons with handmade buttonholes, hook-and-eye closure at waist, white voile double-layer very full skirt with shirring at the waist. To fit doll about 30". 6 1/2" shoulder width. 13" waist. $300/400

27. White Voile Gown
with Lavender Polka Dots
Of very delicate white voile, the gown features a slightly rounded neckline, full bodice with gathers at top of set-in narrow waistband, slightly high-waisted, elbow-length full sleeves achieved by tiny cartridge pleats at the shoulders, constructed sleeve bands, full skirt with cartridge pleating all around, hook-and-eye closure at the back. The dress is trimmed with narrow bands of gathered tulle at the neckline and sleeves. To fit doll about 17". 4" shoulder width. 7" waist. $400/500

28. White/Blue Patterned Cotton Dress
with Shirred Bodice
Of fine white cotton woven with tiny blue flower petals, the dress features a square-cut neckline, bodice formed of five rows of delicate shirring, trumpet-shaped sleeves with width at the underside, set-in waistband above skirt with narrow pleats at the front and cartridge pleating at the back, hook-and-eye and drawstring closure. The sleeves are made of different complementary fabric with large blue pattern, and bands of this different fabric decorate the front of the skirt. The neckline, sleeves and decorative bands are edged with lace. To fit doll about 20". 5" shoulder width. 11" waist. $500/700

29. White Sheer Muslin Gown
Of very fine sheer muslin, the gown features a rounded neckline with self-piping above a fitted bodice overlaid with V-shaped wide bands (the outer band forms a cap over the upper sleeves), set-in waistband with self-piping, four button-and-loop closures at the back, full sleeves with constructed bands, full skirt with cartridge pleating all around, and trimmed by four bands of wide tucking. To fit doll about 12". 3" shoulder width. 6" waist. $300/400

30. Sheer White Dotted Swiss Gown with Attached Overskirt
Of very delicate sheer white dotted Swiss fabric, the gown features a low rounded neckline edged with lace, slightly high waist with full bodice shaped by pleats at neckline and centered by lace bretelles, wide sleeves to the elbow with shoulder gathering and lace edging, full gathered skirt under lace-edged overskirt that is flat-cut at the front and richly bustle-gathered at the back. The dress is trimmed with red-edged coral silk ribbons. To fit doll about 20". 5" shoulder width. 11" waist with drawstring adjustment at the back. $500/700

31. Sheer White Dotted Swiss Gown
Of very finely woven sheer white fabric with interwoven dots, the gown features a low-rounded neckline with wide ruffle collar that nearly covers the short trumpet-shaped sleeves, full bodice with set-in waistband, very full cartridge pleated skirt with wide hem. The collar, neckline and sleeves are lace-edged and there are lavender silk ribbons at the sleeves. To fit slender-bodied doll about 13". 2" shoulder width. 5" waist. $200/300

32. Grey Silk/Woolen Gown with Blue Windowpane Fabric Design
Of very fine grey fabric with narrow windowpane design in dusty blue, the gown features a dart-shaped fitted bodice with slightly dropped shoulders, hook-and-eye closure at the back, long curve-shaped sleeves, full skirt with wide box-pleats all around. The gown is edged in grey and blue silk ribbons and there is a large bow with streamers at the back waist. To fit doll about 20". 5" shoulder width. 10" waist. $300/400

33. Early Dress with Gigot Sleeves and Transfer Design Fabric in Original Box
Of hand-woven cream fabric with transfer design of green leaves and brown squiggles, the dress features a rounded neckline with self-edging, slightly dropped shoulders with self-cording, gigot sleeves formed from cartridge pleats at the shoulders, constructed cuffs with hook-and-eye closures, dart-shaped fully lined bodice with self-cording at the set-in waistband, box-pleated full skirt. The dress is preserved in its early stencil-designed box. To fit doll about 20". 6" shoulder width. 11" waist. $500/700

34. Two Silk Poke Bonnets
Of bronze green or grey silk, the bonnets have gathered sides with set-in plain back, wide brims designed to modestly hide the face. The inside brims are lined with cream lace, and the inside bonnets are shaped with stiffened net. 2" inside head width. $200/250

35. Two Bone-Shaped Bodices
One is of rich brown velvet, the other of brown silk. Each has rounded neckline, slightly dropped shoulders, short sleeves, front center seam that disguises the flat-bone stitched underneath, V-shaped waist, hook-and-eye closure at back. The neckline, shoulders, bottoms of sleeves and waist are edged with self-piping. To fit dolls about 20". 5" shoulder width. 10" waist. $200/300

36. Six Cotton Blouses and Skirts
Each of cotton with delicately printed design in lavender or blue, the six pieces comprise short-sleeved blouse with square-cut neckline and very full bodice with cartridge pleating, and two jackets with open front; along with three skirts, two constructed with flat fronts centered by pleats with cartridge pleating at the back, the larger with cartridge pleating all around. To fit dolls from 12"–20". $400/600

Chapter II:
Fashion Doll Gowns, 1860–1875

detail of back of gown, #37

37. White Pique Gown with Attached Train, and Red Shoes
Of narrow-ribbed white pique the one piece dress is shaped to neatly fit the bodice, waist and hips with ten buttons and handmade buttonholes down the entire length of the front, dropped shoulders with long pagoda-style sleeves, large triangle-shaped pockets from the side-seams, attached dart-shaped bustle at the back with demi-train. The gown is trimmed with self-piping at the neckline and scalloped-edge cutwork at the cuffs, pockets, hem and train. Along with red, soft leather ankle shoes with silk ties, edging, soft leather soles. To fit doll about 23". 4 1/2" shoulder width. 11" waist. 3"l shoes. $500/700

38. Rare Porcelain "Worktable Companion" Doll in Original Costume and Box
8" (20 cm). Pink-tinted porcelain shoulderhead with brown painted hair, kid body with jointed hips and shoulders, painted facial features, blue eyes, red and black eyeliner, closed mouth, blushed cheeks. The lady doll is wearing original white muslin tucked blouse, red flannel skirt with black velvet ribbons trimmed with tiny brass beads, having three pockets containing thimble and needle packets, brown lace-edged velvet cap padded for use as pincushion with gold pins, blue ribbon sash supporting a ball of white thread, black leather belt attached to silver scissors. The doll and a pattern for making it was shown in the Englishwoman's Domestic Magazine for 1860; the needlework doll was described as a "worktable companion". $1500/2000

Drawing of the "Worktable Companion" in the Englishwoman's Domestic magazine, 1860.

39. White Pique Dress with Red Soutache
Of crisp white pique, the dress features a fitted bodice and waist with hook-and-eye closure at the back, wide bretelles at front and back extend into lappets below the waist, V-shaped center bodice, low rounded neckline, very full lantern sleeves formed by double-box-pleats at the shoulders and turned-up bottom edges. The skirt is formed of all-around box pleats. The dress is richly embroidered with red soutache and edged in red cording. Included is a silk snood with red silk ribbon ties. To fit doll about 16". 4" shoulder width. 8" waist. 12" overall length. $800/1000

40. White Pique Dress with White Soutache
Of very narrowly-ribbed pique, the dress features a low-rounded neckline with very wide scalloped edge collar that extends into V-shape at the center front, pagoda-shaped sleeves with scalloped edging, fitted bodice and constructed waist, very full box-pleated skirt with attached scalloped-edge overskirt. The dress is richly embroidered with white soutache and has hook-and-eye closure at the back. To fit doll about 16". 4" shoulder width. 8" waist. 12" overall length. $800/1000

40A. White Pique Gown with Black Soutache
Of very narrowly-ribbed pique, the dress features a low rounded neckline with V-point rolled collar, dart-shaped bodice, constructed waist, hook-and-eye closure at the back, very full box-pleated lantern sleeves with turned up bottom edges, very full box-pleated skirt, detachable sash with bow and streamers at the back. The dress is elaborately trimmed with black soutache. To fit doll about 14". 3 1/2" shoulder width. 8" waist. $500/700

41. White Pique Two-Piece Gown with Bonnet and Shoes
Of very narrowly-ribbed pique the ensemble features a hip-length Basque jacket with fitted torso, low rounded neckline, long trumpet-shaped sleeves, hook-and-eye closure with three decorative buttons at the front, dart-shaped back terminated in box-pleats over the hips. With flat front flared skirt having generous box pleats at the back, attached overskirt that is constructed with flat-front and very full box-pleated vandyked back. The gown is trimmed with very elaborate borders of narrow soutache, cross-stitched banding, and ruffled sheer cotton edged with openwork cotton lace. Included with the gown is grey velvet cap with draped brown velvet band, delicate silk flowers and leaves at inside brim, silk lining. And brown ankle boots with gilt buttons and tiny heels, marked "4". To fit doll about 17". 4" shoulder width. 8" waist. 14" overall length. 2 1/4" shoe length. $1000/1300   2700

42. Extraordinary Album d'Ouvrage of 1884 in Original Wooden Cabinet with 41 Sample Cards
A cabinet-maker quality wooden chest with inlay striping, lock and key, hinges open to reveal shelved interior. Arranged on the shelves are forty-one 9" x 11" cardboard display cards with twill or marbled glazed finish in various colors, each bordered in gilt paper. Each card contains a sample of needlework in miniature form representing various needle arts from sewing to embroidery to fabric repair to making of button holes, or creation of small needlecases or boxes or decoupage-decorated straw ornaments; and each card has small label at the top with decoupage decoration and French description in fine calligraphy handwriting of the work being shown. A sampling of the various 41 cards are shown here; each of the 41 is different and represents various needle skills. One card is dated 1884, and several have the initials "E.D." Known as *Albums d'Ouvrage*, the cabinets of handwork were created at young girl's convent homes during the 19th century; the ability to create minute examples of the needle art being considered a vital aspect of their genteel upbringing. It is unclear whether this album represents the work of one young girl (E.D.?) or is the sample work of the 1884 student body at the French convent. The presentation case and each of its 41 cards are preserved in immaculate condition. $8000/12,000

**43. White Pique High-Waisted Skirt
with Sheer Muslin Blouse**
Of very narrowly-ribbed white pique, the skirt features a very high waistband that virtually forms a bodice, button-and-loop closure at the back, double-box-pleated very full skirt. The skirt is decorated with black soutache, brown silk panels on the bodice, white cotton edging and narrow soutache. With the skirt is a sheer muslin blouse with narrow horizontal tucking, lace collar, long gigot sleeves that are very full at the shoulders, and tapered to fitted lace-edged buttoned cuffs. To fit doll about 16". 4" shoulder width. 8" waist. $600/800

44. Brown Silk Taffeta Gown with Black Velvet Trim
Of crisp brown silk taffeta, the gown features a fitted bodice with V-shaped waist, low rounded collar, flat front skirt with wide pleats, with attached organza short sleeves edged with black velvet over long sleeves with black velvet cuffs and ties. The gown is trimmed with black velvet appliquéd ribbons that extend around the back of the gown. To fit doll about 17". 4" shoulder width. 8" waist. $500/700

45. Mauve and Striped Ecru Silk Gown with Black Lace Trim
Of delicate mauve silk with long sleeves the bodice is attached to an ecru silk overskirt with shaped waist and flared sides, edged with lace and velvet trimmed silk ribbons, and is worn over a longer skirt whose hidden top half is of muslin and whose exposed bottom half is of mauve silk with a double row of diamond-point black lace with velvet edging. To fit doll about 16". 4" shoulder width. 8" waist. $400/500

46. Two Straw Bonnets Known as "Deux Bonjours"
Elaborately woven straw bonnets with beehive-style crowns and upturned brims at front and back are lined with rose cotton and decorated with black velvet bands and zig-zag straw. 1" and 2" inside head width. $300/400

detail of sash, #45

47. Purple and Cream Three-Piece Ensemble in Original Presentation Box
Of beautifully woven purple and cream stripes, the dress features a dart-shaped fitted bodice with button back, full lining, very full sleeves with structured cuffs, buttons and buttonholes. With matching full skirt with narrow pleats and purple silk belt with gilt buckle, along with matching open front jacket with white handmade rick-rack. The ensemble is presented in its original mauve presentation box with early engraving. To fit doll about 16". 4" shoulder width. 8" waist. $700/900

48. Cape and Jacket
The cape is of cream cashmere wool with sleeveless jacket below the long capelet collar, edged with rich purple trim. With mauve and cream striped cotton jacket with pagoda-style sleeves and a double row of purple hand-made rick-rack bordering the jacket front, hem and sleeves. To fit doll about 16". 4" shoulder width. $300/400

49. Purple and Cream Cashmere Wool Gown
Of softest lightweight cashmere wool, the gown features a rounded neck of royal purple edged in handmade rick-rack and box-pleated purple border, long purple sleeves with two rows of rick-rack, fitted bodice, waist, and flat front skirt with purple lower skirt decorated with three borders of purple box pleats centered by white embroidery. There is a sewn-down matching purple belt, and hook-and-eye closures. (Some moth holes at the backside.) To fit doll about 12". 2 1/2" shoulder width. 7" waist. $200/300

50. Lavender Plaid Two-Piece Grenadine Gown
The shadowpane plaid gown in shades of lavender and cream features a jacket with fitted bodice that extends into elegant curves over the hips, coat sleeves with curved shape, along with box-pleated skirt with hook-and-eye closure. The jacket is trimmed with black jet beads that may be a latter addition. To fit doll about 17". 4" shoulder width. 8" waist. $300/400

51

52

54

53

51. White Waffle-Weave Pique Cotton Gown
Of waffle-weave pique cotton, the gown features a low-rounded neck with delicate scalloped edging, fitted bodice with embroidered white cotton bretelles and two bands of narrow braid, short sleeves with matching trim, constructed waist with cord edging, full skirt with flat front centered by pleats that extend all around the gown, cotton ruffle with *pont d'esprit* scalloped edging and two bands of narrow braid at the hem. With three buttons and loops, hook-and-eye closure at waist. To fit doll about 14". 3 1/2" shoulder width. 7" waist. $300/400

52. White Pique Gown with Braid Trim
Of very narrowly-ribbed white pique, the gown features a rounded neckline with self-border, fitted bodice, set-in waistband, trumpet-shaped long sleeves very full at the wrists and having cutwork cotton edging. The dress is decorated with white braid trim at the bodice, cuffs and three rows of trim at the skirt hem. With two button-and-loop closures, and hook-and-eye at the waist. To fit doll about 14". 3" shoulder width. 8" waist. $300/400

53. White Pique Two-Piece Ensemble
Of very narrowly ribbed white pique with interwoven shadow stripe, the two-piece ensemble comprises a flared-side jacket that opens at the front with vandyked bottom edges, having self-fabric cording at neckline, short vandyked sleeves over full-length coat sleeves, two pearl buttons and handmade button holes. With very full box-

detail, #55, #56

pleated skirt with constructed waistband. The gown is trimmed elaborately with three rows of soutache and braid, and the trim pattern is repeated on front and back of jacket, shoulders, cuffs, and skirt. To fit doll about 16". 4" shoulder width. 8" waist. $500/700

54. White Pique Gown with Cotton Ruffles and Overskirt
Of fine narrowly ribbed white pique, the gown features a V-shaped neckline edged with two narrow bands of hand-made rick-rack and scalloped cotton trim; long coat sleeves with matching trim, fitted bodice with hook-and-eye closure. The flat-front skirt has flared sides and an attached overskirt with scalloped-edge cotton ruffle; the overskirt extends around the back where it is richly gathered and longer. The underskirt has a matching scalloped-edge cotton ruffle and gathered back. To fit doll about 16". 4" shoulder width. 8 1/2" waist. $500/700

55. Bronze Silk Bonnet with Lace Edging
Of crisp bronze silk taffeta, the firm-sided bonnet is shaped of elaborately draped wide ribbons, with shaped bows and long streamers, lace-edged brim trimmed with a delicate spray of flowers and stiffened lining. 2" inside head width. $200/300

56. Green Silk Bonnet with Woven Straw Lattice Frame
An open-weave straw bonnet with latticework design and heart-shaped brim is lined with emerald green silk taffeta with a large bow and long streamers; there is a pleated bavolet with black lace edging, and the face is edged with a delicate bouquet of tiny silk flowers and leaves, tulle lining. 2" inside head width. $200/300

57. Black Silk Wired Bonnet with Magenta Velvet Trim
Four wire frames of graduated size form the frame of the black-silk covered bonnet with pleated bavolet. The bonnet is edged with magenta and black velvet, and the inside brim is edged with generous flounces of lace. 2" inside head width. $200/300

58. Royal Blue Silk Bonnet with Black Velvet Trim
The wire-framed bonnet is formed of ice-blue silk with ruffled bavolet, and has black velvet brim and edging. The inside brim is trimmed with Alencon lace, and the bonnet is lined with tulle. 2" inside head width. $200/300

59. Brown Flannel Wool Hat with Aqua Feathers
Of softest brushed flannel with velvety feel, the hat has band and under-brim of aqua brushed flannel, and is banded with delicate aqua feathers and aqua silk satin bow, with stiffened muslin lining. 2" inside head width. $200/300

60. Ivory Silk and Mohair Bonnet
Very luxurious bonnet with long plush mohair cap encircled by wire-framed ivory silk gathered ruffles whose detailed shirring is very evident at the under-brim, with silk lining, and decorated by a spray of shaded-yellow white flowers and leaves. 2" inside head width. $200/300

61. Green Silk Taffeta Skirt with Black Evening Coat
Of emerald green silk taffeta, the skirt has woven pattern at the hem, flat front and narrow pleats all around, with constructed waistband, hook-and-eye closure. Along with white-dotted Swiss long-sleeved blouse with lace-edged collar and cuffs, and with black silk faille evening jacket with delicate black lace edging, coat sleeves with turned up cuffs, shaped collar, two faux-pocket flaps. To fit doll about 17". 4" shoulder width. 8" waist. $300/400

62. Black Velvet Latticework Vest with Velvet Toque
Of rich soft black velvet constructed in open latticework design, the sleeveless vest is edged all around with black scalloped-edge lace. The vest achieves its shape from fitted darts at the backside. Along with black velvet toque with silk lining, and throat band. To fit doll about 17". 4" shoulder width. $300/400

63. Two-Piece Green and Black Silk Ensemble with Bonnet
The blouse of black silk with lace and velvet edging has fitted bodice, long sleeves with double row of lace at cuffs. Along with green skirt with flat front, flared sides, gathers at back waist giving fullness to extended-length skirt back, black velvet ribbon trim. With green flowered-print silk bonnet with tulle lining. To fit doll about 15". 3 1/2" shoulder width. 7 1/2" waist. $300/400

64. Brown Lightweight Woolen Two-Piece Suit
Of very fine lightweight wool, the ensemble features a fitted jacket with dark-shaping at front and back, long sleeves slightly widened at the wrists, round collar with black edging and stand-up scalloped lace collar, flat front brown overskirt with elaborately constructed bustle back, black muslin underskirt with triple rows of scalloped silk ruffles, black piping trim with black silk ribbons. Included is ivory silk parasol with fringed edges, on carved bone handle. To fit doll about 17". 3 1/2" shoulder width. 8" waist. $500/700

65. Silk Plaid Gown
with Velvet Trim and White Blouse
Of blue/red and ivory silk, the gown features a wide waistband that actually forms a bodice, wide straps, constructed waist, wide box-pleated skirt that forms into very tight gathers at the back. The gown has hook-and-eye closures and is trimmed with black velvet bands. There is a white batiste cotton blouse with inset embroidered and lace trim, rounded collar and fitted cuffs with delicate lace edging. To fit doll about 15". 3 1/2" shoulders. 7" waist. $400/500

66. Black Velvet Jacket and Velvet Toque
Of softest black velvet, the short jacket with rounded edges has long sleeves slightly widened at the wrists, and is edged with black fringe all around. Along with black velvet toque with structured shape, red feather, stiffened net interior under blue silk lining. 3" shoulder width. 1 1/2" inside head width. $200/300

67. Tulle Shawl and Coiffe
Of stiffened tulle overlaid with flounces of tulle, the accessory set comprises long shaped shawl-collar and coiffe with extended lappets. Each is edged with very delicate lace and have intertwined blue silk ribbons. For doll about 18". $300/400

68. Grey Pressed Flannel
and Blue Velvet Hat
Of pressed-shaped grey flannel with wide brim, the hat brim is edged with blue silk, and there are two bands of blue velvet ribbon and bows trimmed with brown and white feathers, with silk lining. 2" inside head with. $200/300

69. Flowered Blue Print Silk gown with Black Velvet Trim
Of fine silk in very delicate cornflower blue pattern with striped cream bands sprinkled with rose petals, the rounded neck gown features a fitted bodice with self-cording at the neckline and waist, button-and-loop closures, capelet sleeves with organdy sous-sleeves edged with embroidery and lace, and very full box-pleated skirt. The gown is decorated with black velvet banding at the hem, pockets, sleeves, and edging the silk self-sash. To fit doll about 16". 4 1/2" shoulder width. 10" waist. $500/700

70. Brown Silk Taffeta Gown with Extended Train and Straw Bonnet
Of crisp bronze brown silk taffeta, the gown features a fitted bodice with dart-shaping, coat sleeves, rounded neck, constructed waist, gored skirt with flat front that attaches with hook-and-eye closure at the side, very full pleating at the back that forms a bustle shape with extended long train. The gown is decorated with silk rosettes down the front bodice, at shoulders, cuffs and along the entire hemline including the train, fully lined. Along with straw bonnet with graduated width brim decorated with brown and cream silk

ribbons in elaborate draping. To fit doll about 17". 3 1/2" shoulder width. 8" waist. $500/700

71. Brown Silk Jacket with Knit Snood and Leather Workbasket
Of brown silk, the jacket features rounded neck with lace edging, slightly dropped shoulders with self-piping, long sleeves with lace edging at cuffs, hook-and-eye front closure. Along with silk snood having a double row of brown silk border pleats. And with leather workbasket with red lining, cord handle, and contents including miniature awl, thread-winder, thimble, scissors. To fit doll about 17". 3 1/2" shoulder width. $500/700

72. Brown Silk/Woolen Gown and Silk Reticule
Of an interesting fabric with flecked brown on light brown background, the gown features a dart-fitted bodice with set-in waist, rounded neckline with lace edging, slightly dropped shoulders, coat sleeves, seven-panel skirt with gored shape, flat front, pleats at sides, gathers at back with slightly extended train. The gown is trimmed with coral silk banding at bodice and sleeves and little bows at the shoulders. Along with straw-bottom silk reticule. To fit doll about 17". 3 1/2" shoulder width. 8" waist. $400/500

73. Deep Rose Silk Gown with White Blouse and Muslin Cap
A richly colored deep rose silk is featured on the gown with rounded neckline, self-piping, short sleeves, fitted bodice with constructed waist, gored skirt with flat front and side panels, gathering at the back, hook-and-eye closures at the back with silk bow at the waist; the skirt is trimmed with five bands of darker rose silk ribbons and ivory fringe. Along with white cotton blouse with collar, tucks, buttons and buttonholes, beautifully shaped cuffs. And sheer muslin cap with pleated tulle edging and silk streamers. To fit doll about 16". 4" shoulders. 8" waist. $400/500

74. Three White Blouses
Comprising sheer muslin blouse with vertical tucks and two rows of lace, lace edging at neckline and cuffs, and fine batiste blouse with six very narrow bands of tucking centering a floral-embroidered front panel; with double-ruffle lace collar, long sleeves with embroidered cuffs edged by lace on either edge; button back, and white cotton sacque with multi-rows of lace, cutwork and embroidery on front and at the cuffs. To fit doll about 16". $400/500 *925*

37

75. Rose Silk Two Piece-Gown with Bonnet and Fan
Of soft rose silk, the gown features a bodice with low-rounded neckline, short sleeves, rose silk twill skirt with flat front, side pleats, gathered back with slightly extended train, constructed waist band. Along with straw bonnet trimmed with rose silk bows and silk flowers. And with carved bone folding fan with painted gold and silver designs and intertwined with rose silk ribbons, gilt handle. To fit doll about 16". 4" shoulder width. 8" waist. $700/900

76. Woven Red Straw Bonnet with Rose Taffeta Ribbons
Slightly rounded bonnet woven of red straw is designed to fit against the back of head, richly draped with rose coral ribbons edged with black silk striping, large bow at the back, with silk lining. For doll about 16"–17". $300/400

77. Brown Brocade Gown with White Blouse and Straw Bonnet
Of heavy textured brown brocade with fitted bodice edged with black velvet, hook-and-eye closure at the back bodice, full skirt formed from wide pleats. With white cotton blouse have delicately turned collar with cutwork and scalloped edging. And straw bonnet with patterned woven silk banding, muslin lining. For doll about 14". 3" shoulder width. 8" waist. $300/400

78. Bronze Silk Two-Piece Gown with Straw Bonnet
Of bronze silk taffeta, the two-piece gown features a fitted jacket with flared hip-length sides, dart-shaping, rounded neckline, short capelet sleeves over long trumpet shaped sleeves; with full skirt having flat front, box pleats at the sides and cartridge gathers at the back. There is very narrow aqua silk piping at neckline and jacket hem. Along with straw bonnet with draped aqua silk ribbons banding and fabric rose petals. To fit doll about 16". 4" shoulder width. 8" waist. $300/400

79. Brown Plush Velvet Hat with Aqua Silk Trim
Of very soft combed velvet plush, the rounded top hat has wire-framed brim of graduated width, aqua silk shirred lining of under brim, aqua silk ribbons with large blue feather, silver medallion, stiffened net with silk lining. 2" inside head with. $300/400

detail, #79

80. White Mull and Muslin Two-Piece Gown with Wide Alencon Lace Borders and Cap
Of sheer white mull the two-piece gown features a dart-fitted jacket. V-shaped neckline with buttoned front, long sleeves with pagoda-style sleeves, box-pleated bands edge the jacket hem and sleeves, and there is lace at the collar. The jacket is partially lined for modesty. With sheer muslin skirt having flat front and very full gathered back, decorated with two wide borders of lace, over muslin underskirt with lace border. Along with woven openwork cap with tulle ruffle, long silk streamers. To fit doll about 14". 3" shoulder width. 7" waist. $400/500

81. White Dotted Swiss Two-Piece Gown with Ruffled Front
Of white dotted Swiss with shaped loosely-fitted jacket having front closure and edged by a row of lace-edged ruffles that extend entirely down the front and around the bottom of the jacket to the fitted back, slightly dropped shoulders, piping at neckline. With matching full skirt having all-around gathers and set-in waistband. To fit doll about 18". 4 1/2" shoulder width. 9" waist. $500/700   950

82. Brown Velvet Toque and Black Leather Heeled Shoes
Of brown velvet, the toque features a double row of brown banding, cream silk lining. Along with black leather fashion shoes with silver buckles, brown soles, tiny heels. 1 1/2" inside head width. 2" shoes. $200/300

83. Organza Cream Gown with Muslin Undergown
Of most delicate organza, the gown features a fitted muslin-under-organza bodice with square-cut neckline, fitted muslin sleeves with pouf organza sleeves, gore-shaped muslin skirt with bustle-shaped back having extended train; the muslin skirt has two wide ruffles of sheer net at the hemline, and an overskirt of organza with shirred detailing. The gown is trimmed with cotton lace and rose silk bows with rose petal. To fit doll about 15". 3 1/2" shoulder width. 7" waist. $500/700

84. Fine Cream Cotton Gown with Elaborate Bustle
Of finely woven cream cotton, the flat-front gown with shaped but unstructured front waist features ten narrow vertical tucks down the entire front, centered by very wide bands of lace; bands of tucking and lace alternate all around the back of the dress. There are hook-and-eye closures and constructed waist at the back, rounded collar with button and loop at back neck and lace edging. The very full back skirt is formed from deep pleats that create a bustle, two borders of lace edge the hemline, and there is an extended train. To fit doll about 15". 3 1/2" shoulder width. 7" waist. $500/600

85. Changeable Silk Taffeta Gown and Cape
Of purple/blue changeable color silk taffeta, the gown features a fitted bodice with hook-and-eye front closure, long sleeves with ruffled detail at shoulders and cuffs, lace trim at neckline and cuffs, long flared skirt with ruffled detail at the hem, attached overskirt with ruffled border and pleated bustle back with bow and streamers. Included is ruffled border matching cape. To fit doll about 15". 3" shoulder width. 7" waist. $300/400

86. Claret Silk Taffeta Two-Piece Gown
Of claret-colored silk taffeta, the two-piece gown features a fitted jacket with rounded neckline trimmed with self-piping, faux-button front with hidden hook-and-eye closure, slightly dropped shoulders with long sleeves having wide ruffle trim at the wrists that gives the illusion of constructed cuffs, ruffled jacket hem that gathers into a flounce at the back waist; with matching flat-front skirt gathered at the back and with overskirt with bustle back and pleated ruffle. With black buttons and black silk ribbons. To fit doll about 17". 4" shoulder width. 8" waist. $400/500

87. Claret Silk Two-Piece Fashion Gown
Of soft claret silk satin, the slender-bodied gown features a long dart-fitted jacket that extends below the hips at the side flaps, forms a V-front, and is covered by generous wide bows at the back. The neckline and cuffs of long fitted sleeves are edged with sewn-on box pleats and lace, and the skirt has flat box pleats at the front, gathers at the back, and ruffled trim on the skirt. To fit doll about 21". 5" shoulder width. 10" waist. $600/800

88. Burgundy Silk Two-Piece Fashion Gown
Of lustrous burgundy silk, the two-piece gown features a long-waisted jacket with lappets, and inset plastron of red silk tucks; the jacket flares and fits snugly over the hips with red box pleats at the back waist. With rounded collar, long sleeves very full at the shoulders with wide cuffs, pleated front skirt, very full gathered back skirt with slightly extended length. To fit doll about 21". 5" shoulder width. 9" waist. $500/700

detail, #87

detail, #88

44

89. Grey/Silver Striped Silk Gown with Black Velvet Trim
Of crisp silk in narrow stripes of grey and silver, the two-piece gown features fitted jacket with back extending over the full gathered skirt. The jacket has V-shaped neckline edged with black lace that is repeated on the cuffs of long sleeves, and lappets that extend over the shoulders and are edged in black velvet ribbons that also appear on cuffs and jacket front opening. The full skirt features a flat front and very full back with extended train, and is decorated with bands of black velvet ribbon and wide silk bands of the grey/silver fabric formed into ribbons and edged with the narrow black velvet ribbons. To fit doll about 18". 4" shoulder width. 8" waist. $700/900

90. Petite Grey Silk/Linen Gown with Black Velvet Trim
The two-piece ensemble of grey silk/linen features a waist-length jacket with dart-shaping at front and back, rounded neckline edged with black velvet and lace, 3/4 sleeves with black velvet cuffs, and a flat-front skirt with very full pleats at the back. The costume is trimmed with black velvet bands, lace and grey silk edging. To fit doll about 11". 3" shoulder width. 7" waist. $200/300

91. Black/White Plaid Silk Two-Piece Gown with Blue Silk Trim
Of black and white silk (some frailty), the gown features a dart-shaped hip-length jacket with black button front, V-shaped neckline with blue box-pleated collar, flat-front skirt with very full back and modified bustle formed by gathers. The skirt is edged by four rows of box pleats in alternate patterns of black and white plaid, and ice blue silk and edged by blue braid. The cuffs are edged by blue box pleats and two rows of blue braid, and there are two generous blue silk bows at the back jacket. To fit doll about 14". 4" shoulder width. 8" waist. 300/400

92. Brown Silk/Linen Two-Piece Gown with Red Ribbon Trim
Of richly woven brown silk/linen, the gown features a fitted jacket that flares over the hips extending to V points at front and back, slightly dropped shoulders, long coat-shaped sleeves, rounded collar; and matching flat-front skirt with very full box-pleated back. The gown is trimmed with red appliqué ribbons and lace edging at neckline and cuffs. To fit doll about 15". 3 1/2". 8" waist. $500/700

93. Petite Dark Brown Woolen Fashion Gown
Of finely woven lightweight wool, the one-piece gown features dart-shaped fitted flat front with button closure, flared sides, constructed back waist below sewn-down pleats and forming into very full pleats at the back skirt. The skirt features a demi-train and is edged all-around by a wide border of narrow pleats. There are two pleated pockets and the gown is edged with lace at the neckline and cuffs. To fit doll about 12". 2" shoulder width. 6" waist. $300/400

94. Brown/Purple Plaid Woolen Gown with Velvet Trim
Of shaded purple and brown plaid, the one-piece gown features loosely fitted flat front with flared sides, dart-shaped back with demi-train, velvet rolled collar and turn-up cuffs, front opening trimmed with four black velvet ribbons, black buttons and handmade buttonholes. Along with black lace bonnet trimmed with velvet mauve ribbons and flowers. To fit doll about 15". 4" shoulder width. 9" waist. $400/500

95. Burgundy Wool and Silk Two-Piece Fashion Gown and Straw Bonnet
Of fine burgundy wool, the two-piece gown features dart-shaped jacket having burgundy silk pleated front with hidden hook-and-eye closure at center front, dart-shaped back, lace-edging at collar and cuffs, burgundy silk edging at bottom edge of jacket. The skirt features a flat-front of burgundy silk overlaid by diagonally wrapped wool overskirt with three full-length pleats, and a woolen underskirt with wool pleats edging the hemline, and very full overskirt captured by center stitched tucks. There is a narrow pleated net ruffle at the neckline and cuffs. Along with straw with silk ribbon and organza trim. To fit doll about 21". 5" shoulder width. 9" waist. $700/900

96. Blue Woolen Two-Piece Gown with Velvet Trim and Velvet Bonnet
Of lightweight navy blue wool, the gown features a hip-length jacket with dart-shaping at front and back, velvet front panels centering the lace-edged opening with gilt buttons and handmade buttonholes, long sleeves with velvet cuffs and lace edging. With blue woolen skirt with horizontally draped pleats bordered by blue velvet panels, four rows of box pleats at the hem, bustle-shaped overskirt at the back. Along with patterned blue velvet bonnet trimmed with navy blue silk banding, white feather, ivory silk lining. To fit doll about 17". 4" shoulder width. 7" waist. $700/900

97. Red Cotton Two-Piece Gown with White Embroidery
Of red cotton, the two-piece gown features dart-shaped blouse with rounded neckline edged in red-embroidered ribbon, dropped shoulders with ribbon edging and very wide ruffled sleeves with scalloped edging and feathered embroidery, matching ruffled trim at hips, eight decorative pearl buttons, hook-and-eye closure. With cartridge pleated full skirt having two wide embroidered ruffles at the hem. To fit doll about 22". 5" shoulder width. 11" waist. $400/500

98. Blue Striped Two-Piece Fashion Gown
Of striped cotton in shades of blue, ecru and rose, the two-piece gown features very long jacket with button front, rounded collar with lace-edging, 3/4 sleeves, button front, two pockets with lace-edging and pearl buttons, box-pleated back with long lace-edged ties, flat-front skirt with gathered back, ruffled detail at the hem. To fit doll about 16". 4" shoulder width. 9" waist. $400/500

99. Linen Dress with Cutwork Trim
Of natural linen the dress features rounded neckline, princess shaping with jacket-style trim, flared skirt back, button front with wooden buttons and handmade buttonholes, coat sleeves. The dress is richly trimmed with embroidered bands of cutwork around the neckline, cuffs, hem, and faux-jacket edges forming a flounce at the back of the skirt, with three curved strips of white braid down the entire back. To fit doll about 15". 4" shoulder width. 11" overall length. $400/500

100. A Collection of 41 Patterns for French Poupees
The 41 large tissue sheets from Le Journal des Enfants features costumes from the 1880's, specifically designed for poupees, size 4, or bebes, size 1, including dresses, hats, party costumes, gowns and accessories. Each is detailed with excellent illustrations and various views of each object. 15" x 22" sheets, $600/900

Chapter III:
Bebe Dresses, 1875–1895

101. White Pique Princess-Style Dress and Bonnet
Of fine white pique, the button front dress features princess shaping, middy-style collar with cutwork scalloped edging, coat sleeves with embroidered faux-cuffs. The dress is decorated with generous scalloped-edge borders of cutwork and embroidery on either side of the button front, box-pleated border at the hem below two other borders of similar embroidery. Along with white pique bonnet with box-pleated bavolet edged in cutwork and embroidery, cotton box-pleating framing the face with tatting edge, cluster of silk ribbons at the crown, silk lining. To fit doll about 23". 5" shoulder width. 15" overall length. $600/800

102. White Pique Princess-Style Dress and Bonnet
Of fine white pique, the button front dress features princess shaping, rounded neckline with self banding, 12 pearl buttons and handmade buttonholes, dropped shoulders, coat sleeves, two large rounded pockets, dart-shaped jacket-style back with

detail, #102

detail, #103

buttoned flaps over pleated skirt. The dress is trimmed with embroidered scalloped edge cutwork borders and at cuffs, pocket edges, back collar, and back jacket flaps. Along with cream bonnet with box-pleated bavolet, wire-framed ruffles frame the face, ecru silk ribbons. To fit doll about 32". 7" shoulder width. 21" overall length. $500/700

103. White Princess-Style Dress and Silk-Edged Lace Coiffe
Of textured white cotton, the princess-style dress features a rounded neckline, slightly dropped shoulders, coat sleeves with faux-turned-up cuffs, detail at back of dress includes middy-shaped collar and vandyked tails above seventeen pleats. The dress is edged around the collar, down each side of the pearl button front, around the skirt hem and tails, and cuffs with a border of handmade cutwork and embroidery. Included with the dress is a lace coiffe bordered with wide ruffled blue ribbons and streamers. To fit doll about 18". 4 1/2" shoulder width. $600/800

104. White Waffle-Weave Cotton Dress with Scottish Tam and Leather Boots
Of white textured waffle-weave cotton, the princess-style dress features a rounded neck with white cotton cording, button front with four pearl buttons and buttonholes, long sleeves, single kick pleat at the back. The dress is edged in cotton lace down the front and entire hem, and cuffs. Along with Scottish tam of fine lightweight wool, trimmed with velvet band and soutache trim, black feather, sateen lining. And leather ankle boots with gold buttons, leather undersoles, tiny wooden heels, marked "J" or "O". To fit doll about 12". 2 1/2" shoulder width. $400/500

106. White Cotton Dress with Soutache
Of shadowprint white cotton, the princess-style dress features rounded neckline, front closure with eight pearl buttons and handmade buttonholes, hip-length bretelles that drape over the very short sleeves with open slits at the top, decorative bands at the lower dress that extend around the entire back. The dress is decorated with soutache embroidery and the collar, sleeves, bretelles, and bands are edged with very fine scalloped edging. To fit doll about 17". 4" shoulder width. $200/300

107. White Cotton Shadowprint Dress with Cutwork Trim
Of finely woven white cotton with shadowprint stripes, the dress features low rounded neckline with self-cording and lace edging, full-length sleeves with constructed cuffs and lace edging, two rows of gathered ruffles with elaborate cutwork at the hem, and six pearl buttons with handmade buttonholes. To fit doll about 20". 5" shoulder width. $200/300

108. White Pique Princess-Style Dress
Of vertically-ribbed white pique the princess-style dress has V-shaped neckline that extends into square-shaped collar at the back, coat sleeves, attached jacket style flaps; the flaps extend around the dress and at the back hips form a vandyked edging over box pleats. The dress is richly ornamented with very fine border and inset handwork, and has five buttons and handmade buttonholes at the front. To fit doll about 15". 3" shoulder width. $300/400

109. Blue Silk Faille Gown with White Blouse and Tulle-Trimmed Straw Bonnet
Of cornflower-blue silk faille, the gown features low square-cut neckline, sleevelets, fitted bodice with slightly high waist, hook-and-eye closure at the back, full skirt with flat front and back pleats, blue velvet edging of collar and sleeves, and three bands of blue velvet ribbon on

105. White Waffle-Weave Jacket
Of white cotton waffle-weave to suggest intricate quilting, the jacket features slightly flared sides, round collar with corded edge above a wide rounded collar with cutwork scalloped cotton edging, long coat sleeves, front opening with hidden hook-and-eye closures, two hip pockets at side seams. The jacket is edged at collar, front, entire hem, pockets and cuffs with scalloped-edge white cotton having cutwork and embroidery detail. To fit doll about 22". 4 1/2" shoulder width. $400/500

the front skirt and along the side and back hem. With white batiste blouse having lace trim at neckline and cuffs. And with straw bonnet wrapped in gathered tulle at upper and lower brims, and capped with a flounce of tulle, blue silk ribbons and flowers, blue silk edging, muslin lining. To fit doll about 21". 5" shoulder width. 12" waist. $800/1000

110. White Fur Collar and Muff in Original Boxes
White fur collar with foxtail trim and (very frail) blue silk padded lining, along with matching muff with blue silk tassels. Each is preserved in its original green paper box shaped to fit. For doll about 16". $400/500

111. Rose Silk Bodice
Of very tiny patterned rose silk checkered print, the bodice features a rounded neckline edged with a box-pleated ribbon border, dart-shaping curving into bone-backed V-shaped waist, short sleeves with matching trim to neckline, rose ribbon rosettes at sleeves and center bodice, lacing at back. To fit doll about 35". 11" shoulder width. $300/400

112. Brown Linen/Silk Bodice with Blue Ribbon Trim
Of brown linen with interwoven silk stripes, the bodice features a rounded neckline with button front, short trumpet sleeves, dart shaping at front and back with dropped back waist. The fully lined bodice has box pleats at sleeve and waist edges, and is trimmed with blue ribbon banding, neckline lace, blue covered buttons, and three large silk rosettes. To fit doll about 35". 11" shoulder width. $400/500

113. Blue Silk Bodice with Silver Buttons
Of ice blue silk with very narrow black stripes, the square neck bodice features button front with handmade buttonholes and floral shaped silver buttons, scalloped edge gathered sleevelets, extended length back shaped at the waist. The bodice is trimmed with wide scalloped edge bands of self-fabric and has two bows at the shoulders and back. To fit doll about 35". 11" shoulder width. $300/400

114. White Pique Jacket
Of narrowly-ribbed white pique, the short jacket features square cut neckline and angle-shaped front, dart-shaped back with detailed flaps at the back, sleevelets. The jacket is edged with scalloped edge cutwork and embroidered with soutache. To fit doll about 30". 9" shoulder width. $200/300

115. White Fur Collar and Muff in Original Boxes
Of lush white fur, lined with padded blue silk (worn on muff) the set includes shaped collar, and muff with tassel neck cord. Each is preserved in its original green paper box shaped to fit. To fit doll about 24". $400/500

116. Blue Silk Princess-Styled Dress and Tulle Bonnet
Of ice blue silk, the princess-styled dress has 14 pearl buttons with handmade buttonholes, dropped waist with unusual V-shaped hips, long coat sleeves with turned-up cuffs, blue silk lower skirt with a wide band of ruching above box pleats at the front, box pleats at the back, dart-shaped back torso. The dress is extravagantly trimmed with wide borders of cutwork that extend to form pleated draping over the hips, and there is a blue silk sash that ties at the front and a dramatically large blue silk bow at the back. Along with tulle bonnet box-pleated tulle edging and lavish silk ribbon frou-frou at the crown. Originally a child's dress, it would appropriately fit a doll about 38". 8" shoulder width. $700/900

117. Child's Blue Leather Ankle Boots in Original Box
Of robin's egg blue very soft leather, the ankle boots feature curved top, scalloped flaps with seven buttons and buttonholes, canvas lining with white kid leather inside edging, soft leather soles, shaped heels, preserved in original box of shoe-maker, Maison Philippe Latour of Paris. 6 1/2"l shoes. $200/300

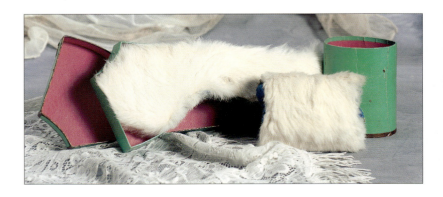

118. Rich Purple Silk Gown with White Blouse and Ruffled Bonnet
Purple silk gown features bodice with bretelle straps, set-in waistband, full skirt with box pleats all-around, black lace edging and trim; with white voile blouse having lace-edged low neckline, long sleeves with lace and embroidered cuffs. Along with white cotton bonnet with exquisite tiny embroidery, tucks, and four rows of gathered lace framing the face, long cotton streamers. To fit child doll about 22". 6" shoulder width. 10" waist. $500/700

119. Four Pairs of Leather Gloves
Of fine kid leather with scalloped or bounded edging, separated fingers and stitched-on thumbs, including two pairs of cream kid with light tan overcast stitching and pearl buttons and buttonholes at wrists; and two simpler pairs of mauve or brown kid. Largest pair 4 1/2"l. $500/700

120. Lavender Striped Silk Dress
Of lavender silk taffeta the dress features a dropped waist with button front, handmade buttonholes, vibrant purple buttons, mauve silk hip sash, double row of gathered pleats below the hips, coat sleeves with ruffled detail at cuffs, lace edging at cuffs and neckline. To fit doll about 19". 4 1/2" shoulder width. 13" overall length. $400/500

121. Grey Silk Dress with Mauve Taffeta Silk Trim
Of grey shantung silk with dropped waist, wide four-pleat hip sash, rounded neckline, sleeves to below the elbows, narrow pleats from below the hips, mauve taffeta pleated plastron and cuffs, lace edging at cuffs and neckline, dart-shaped back adorned with wide mauve silk bow. To fit doll about 19". 4" shoulder width. 13" overall length. $300/400

122. Burgundy Maroon Silk Princess-Style Dress and Straw Bonnet
Of crisp burgundy silk taffeta with well-fitted princess shaping, the dress features low rounded neckline, long sleeves, pleated silk sash around the hips, box-pleating below the sash, buttoned back, and trimmed with lace at the neckline, cuffs,

hem and forming decorative bands at the front and back of dress. Along with three-color woven straw bonnet with burgundy silk banding and generously shirred under brim. To fit doll about 17". 4" shoulder width. 12" overall length. $500/700

123. Purple Silk Taffeta Princess-Style Dress
Of vibrant light-shaded purple silk taffeta, the princess-styled dress has front closure with four pearl buttons and handmade button holes, pleated hip sash with large bow at the dart-shaped back, coat sleeves, cream cotton wide collar and cuffs with lace edging. Along with straw bonnet richly decorated with cream ribbons and silk gathered underbrim. To fit doll about 15". 4" shoulder width. 10" overall length. $400/500

58

124. Ivory Silk Faille Bonnet with Lace Borders
Of rich ivory silk faille with circular bands of ruching at the back centering a lace circlet, the bonnet is framed with extravagant borders of pleated lace, frou-frou, wide ruffled lace border and generous ivory silk ribbons. 4" inside head with. $300/400

125. Ivory Silk Gathered Bonnet with Organza Ruffle
Of ivory silk, the bonnet back has center medallion of silk and lace bordered by richly gathered circle, with overlay of lace and ruffles of silk, lace and organza framing the lace and forming a bavolet. 4" inside head width. $200/300

126. Ivory Silk Satin Bonnet with Organza
A full and lavishly gathered organza back is bordered by a wide band of ivory silk satin, with wire-frame encircling the face and overlaid with elaborately gathered tulle, and frou-frou ivory silk ribbons. 4" inside head width. $300/400

127. Silk Plisse Bonnet with Lace Trim
Of fine ivory silk plisse the bonnet back is shaped by vertical band of shirring off-setting two gathered bonnet wings, wide band with ivory silk ribbons, elaborate silk frou-frou, tulle, and wide lace trim decorated the silk plisse ruffled border. 4 1/2" inside head width. $300/400

127A. Tiny Burgundy Silk Taffeta Dress and Straw Bonnet
Of crisp burgundy silk taffeta the princess-styled dress has shirred silk hip sash with lace trim, and two rows of ruffled lace at the skirt bottom, rounded neckline with self-banding, lace edged neckline and sleevelet edges. Along with wide-brimmed straw bonnet generously decorated with ivory silk ribbons and silk flowers. To fit doll about 7". 2" shoulder width. 4" overall length. $400/500

128. Burgundy and Plaid Silk Dress with Lace Trim, with Ivory Silk Bonnet
Elaborately constructed dress features inset front silk panel with alternating bands of shirring and gathers and overlaid by three sets of plaid silk flaps with hook-and-eye closures, constructed hip band above burgundy silk pleats, long coat sleeves with widened wrists, very wide collar that extends entirely around the back. The back of dress is of plaid silk with rich shirring at center plaid panel outlined with burgundy cording. The dress is trimmed with very wide borders of fine lace, long ruffled lace cuffs, and burgundy silk bows. Along with ivory silk satin bonnet with wire shaped frame, silk lining, and elaborate lace ruffled borders. To fit doll about 23". 5" shoulder width. 15" overall length. $1100/1400

129. Maroon Wool Dress with Princess Styling and Tri-Color Straw Bonnet
Of maroon lightweight wool (with moth holes), the shaped dress features insert plastron of peach silk with cartridge pleating at the top and peach ribbons at the front hips, peach silk collar, double rows of narrow wool pleating below the hips in the front, and topped by a pleated hip sash with gathered bustle at the back, long sleeves with lace edging. Along with tri-color straw bonnet with maroon velvet ribbons, the under-brim is lined with pleated velvet. To fit doll about 18". 4 1/2" shoulder width. 12" overall length. $400/500

130. Burgundy Wool and Brocade Dress with Velvet Bonnet
The dropped waist dress features front and back panels of pleated fine lightweight wool in narrow pleats with defined waist shape at the back, with silk brocade coat sleeves and middy collar. The detachable skirt is constructed of alternate bands of wool and silk with final lower band of narrowly-pleated brocade. The dress has silk covered buttons, jacket edging and faux pocket flaps. Along with wire-framed burgundy velvet hat with graduated width brim, trimmed lavishly with ivory silk bands and ribbons, ivory silk lining. To fit doll about 22". 5 1/2" shoulder width. 13" overall length. $500/700

130A. Woven Straw Sunbonnet with Velvet Back
Of very finely woven dark straw, the bonnet is shaped with deep sides to completely shadow the face, with firm-shaped velvet-covered back, velvet at back sides and along the bottom edge, organza lined interior brim with gathered detail at outer edge. With decorative rose-shaded-ivory ribbons. Inside head width 3 1/2". 6" depth. $300/400

131. Maroon Velvet and Silk Dress with Velvet-Trimmed Straw Bonnet
The rich maroon velvet jacket dress features hip-length jacket open at the front with inserted red silk plastron, attached to red silk pleated skirt, coat sleeves with wide band of upturned lace cuffs. Along with two-color straw bonnet with maroon silk ribbons. To fit doll about 20". 5" shoulder width. 13" overall length. $600/900

132. Burgundy Woolen Dress and Lace Bonnet
Of fine lightweight burgundy wool, the dress features dropped waist with sewn-down tucks at front panel edged with scalloped lace, lace collar, decorative brass buttons, wide pleated hip sash with lace edging and burgundy silk bow at the back, pleated lower skirt, dart-shaped back with brass button closure, long coat sleeves with pleated draping at lace-edged cuffs. Along with fine embroidered tulle bonnet with box-pleated border at neck, and two box-pleated borders framing the face, interwoven with silk frou-frou. To fit doll about 16". 3 1/2" shoulder width. 10" overall length. $500/700

132A. Hat, Shoes and Gloves for Small Doll
Comprising tan leather shoes with ankle straps, silver button closure, overcast edging, leather soles stamped "2" and "made in Germany" in the exact style of French bebe shoes; along with white straw bonnet with unusual double brim, richly decorated with brown silk faille banding, brown and white features and rosebuds' and white kid gloves with overcast stitching on fingers. 1 1/4"l shoes. 2" inside head width. $400/500

134. Straw Bonnet with Coral Silk Ribbons
The flat-topped bonnet with brim upturned all around is richly decorated with wide black-edged coral ribbon forming bands and bows, and punctuated by a spray of magenta silk flowers. Coral silk bows appear on the inside brim, and the bonnet is muslin lined. 3" inside head with. $300/400

135. Very Fine Woven Bonnet in Original Labeled Box
Of gold metallic stiffened thread for shaping, the bonnet is trimmed with silk ruffles at the crown and has cotton lace and silk ribbons framing the lace, with silk lining and streamers. The bonnet has original milliner's label inside the head for Maison Escarre, and is contained in its original box with Maison Escarre label on the exterior. 4 1/2" inside head width. $400/500

136. Lace Bonnet in Original Box from Grand Magasins du Louvre
Stiffened tulle bonnet with interwoven silk flecks is decorated with rolled silk ribbon bands that meet at the back of head and form a ribbon rosette; with wide lace ruffles framing the face, interspersed with silk ribbon frou-frou and crested by a silk ribbon rosette. The bonnet is presented in its original box from Grand Magasins du Louvre, the Paris department store. To fit doll about 4" head width. $300/400

133. Brown Velvet Princess-Style Dress
Of soft brown velvet, the princess-style shaped dress has rounded neckline, coat sleeves extending to below the elbows, button front with eight buttons and handmade buttonholes, two pockets, dart-shaped back with box pleats below the back waist. The dress is trimmed at neckline and cuffs with coral silk and lace, the pockets are edged with coral silk and bows, and there are two generous coral silk bows at the back hips. To fit doll about 18". 5" shoulder width. 12" overall length. $400/500

137. Large Back Velvet Dress and Brushed Velvet Bonnet
Of luxurious black velvet, the coat-shaped dress with dropped waist features double row of pearl buttons down the front, velvet flaps over ivory silk pleated lower skirt, dart-shaping at back, coat sleeves, double collar with velvet collar atop ivory silk pleated collar. Along with cream brushed velvet bonnet with wide upturned brim, braid edging, ivory silk twill draped band with double pom-pom centered rosettes, cotton sateen lining. A child's dress originally, the dress will fit doll about 35"–37". 9 1/2" shoulder width. $500/700

138. Ivory Velvet Plush Bonnet
Wire-framed bonnet of lush ivory velvet plush has lavishly draped band of same fabric, silk bows and feather trim, and the under brim is decorated with pleated and shirred ivory silk, muslin lining. 4" inside head width. $300/400

139. Leather Shoes for Bru, Size 7
Of black leather with ankle straps, brown silk banding, black leather bows with oval silver buckle. Brown leather soles marked "Bru Jne Paris" (in oval) and "7". One sole missing. 3 1/2"l. $300/400

140. Leather Shoes for Bru Bebe, Size 0
Of black leather with ankle straps, brown silk banding, black leather bows with silver buckle. Brown leather soles marked "Bru Jne Paris" (in oval) and "0". 1 1/2"l. $400/500

141. Leather Shoes for Bru Bebe, Size 4
Of black leather with ankle straps, brown silk banding. Brown leather soles marked "Bru Jne Paris" (in oval) and "4". Leather bows missing. 2"l. $200/250

142. Child's Mid-19th Century Sewing Box
A heavy card box with colorfully lithographed lid depicting children tumbling over a vegetable basket, has fitted interior with miniature spools of thread, little boxes with lithograph designs containing tiny buttons, and various sewing implements including scissors, tiny brass thimble, needles, and bone awl and hook. 5 1/2" x 4".

143. Petite Blue Cotton Dress with Straw Bonnet and Red Purse
Of navy blue cotton, the dropped waist dress features two ruffles below the hips, cartridge pleating at center bodice, square cut neckline, short sleeves, lace and ribbon trim. And straw bonnet with ivory silk satin band, bow and lining. And red leather purse with a number of calling cards for "Mlle. Louise". To fit doll about 7". 2" shoulder width. $500/700

144. Royal Blue Silk Dress and Ivory Plush Velvet Bonnet
Of royal blue silk, the dress features jacket top with aqua plastron, edged by fine scalloped lace that also forms a collar. The dart-shaped jacket back has tails under very ornately draped blue silk bow, the sleeves are edged with lace cuffs, and the jacket is lined with aqua silk. The jacket is attached in dress form to a front skirt panel of aqua silk under lace, and a back skirt of royal blue pleats. Along with ivory brushed velvet plush bonnet with plush draped banding and decorated with white feather and ivory silk bow, with gathered silk under brim and muslin lining. To fit doll about 25". 5" shoulder width. 16" overall length. $2000/2500

145. Navy Blue Princess-Style Dress with Bonnet and Muff
Of very tightly woven linen-like fabric the princess-styled dress features eleven handmade buttonholes and little black buttons centered down the front of the dress and highlighted by a black silk V-shaped ribbon sash. There is a matching sash at the hips that forms a large bow at the back and two gathered skirt ruffles with pleated muslin underskirt, and 3/4 coat sleeves with black silk cuffs. There is lace edging at neckline and cuffs. Included with the ensemble are a straw bonnet (some straw wear at edges) with black velvet trim and black silk lining, and a grey lambswool muff with black velvet edging. To fit doll about 20". 4 1/2" shoulder width. 12" overall length. $300/400

146. Black Velvet and Silk Dress and Black Velvet Bonnet
The princess-style dress features black velvet bodice with wide pleated hip sash of black silk twill, printed with tiny colorful flowers and terminating in a very large bow at back hips; above narrow black silk pleats, hook-and-eye front opening, black velvet sleeves with black twill cuffs, patterned black twill collar and three front bows, lace trim at neckline and cuffs. Along with black straw bonnet with wide brim decorated with black feather and silk bows, and lined with black velvet. To fit doll about 20". 4" shoulder width. 13" overall. $700/1000

147. Black Leather Shoes with Charles Morrell Label
Of black leather with light brown overcast edging around the ankle straps, black scalloped edge bows with oval silver buckle.

Leather sole with original paper label of the London shop of Charles Morrell. One sole missing. 2 1/4"l. $200/250

148. Midnight Blue Velvet Dress and Bonnet
Of richest midnight blue velvet, the jacket-style dress features richly gathered red silk plastron with ruching at the yoke, lace edged lapels with red piping that extends to form a wide collar at the back, wide red silk hip sash above box-pleated skirt with lace-edged underskirt; two extended tails at the back. The sleeves are edged with red piping and lace. Along with a wire-framed blue velvet bonnet with red silk lining, banding, bows and a red feather attached with metal ornament (bonnet lining is very frail). To fit doll about 18". 4" shoulder width. 12" overall length. $500/600

149. Midnight Brown Textured Velvet Coat Dress and Bonnet

An unusual checkerboard weave of darkest brown velvet features box pleats down the front with hidden hook-and-eye closure and a shaped attached sash with decorative silver buckle. The dress back features dart-shaped top above a gathered skirt. With 3/4 coat sleeves and lace-edged collar. Included is midnight brown velvet bonnet with wire frame, silk lining, and vibrant red silk ribbons. To fit doll about 19". 5" shoulder width. 13" overall length. $500/700

150. Two-Color Straw Beehive Bonnet

Of silver grey and natural straw with very high beehive-shaped bone encircled by wide brim with upturned side brim, the bonnet is decorated with red silk and navy silk faille ribbons, and has draped red silk lining on the inside brim. 2" inside width. 4" overall width. $200/300

151. Black Velvet Bonnet with Milliner's Label

Designed to frame the face, the black velvet bonnet has graduated size brim very wide at the top and edged with delicate feathers. The bonnet back is banded with black velvet ribbons and trimmed with fabric flowers and leaves. With black muslin lining, Philadelphia milliner's label, and black velvet ribbons. Inside head circumference 4". $200/300

152. Aqua Silk Brocade Dress and Bonnet
A princess-style dress of floral-patterned aqua silk brocade with self-cording at neck and hemline, delicate cream organza insert that extends the full front length and is bordered by green silk ribbon, dart-shaped back, knife-pleated border at hemline with underhem. Along with aqua silk bonnet with wire frame and self-ruffle, muslin lining. The silk is a bit frail on sleeves and back of bonnet. To fit doll about 18". 4" shoulder width. 12" overall length. $300/400

153. Aqua Silk Faille Princess-Style Dress and Straw Bonnet
Of crisp aqua silk faille the princess-style dress features dart-shaping at the back, hidden hook-and-eye closure at the front behind a row of silk covered buttons, pleated hip sash of ivory silk above a band of vertical knife pleats with lace-edged muslin underskirt. The dress has rounded collar with ivory silk and cotton lace edging, and coat sleeves with similar trim. A woven silk reticule is included along with a woven straw bonnet lined with gathered silk, and decorated with ivory silk bands and streamers. To fit doll about 17". 4" shoulder width. 11" overall length. $600/800

154. Maroon Velvet and Aqua Silk Bonnet
With hidden wire frame to give shape to the rounded bonnet, of richly draped maroon velvet with a double border of pleated aqua silk and draped aqua silk band with silk faille streamers. Cream silk padded lining and trim of black feather and tiny petals. 2 3/4" inside head width. 3 1/2" overall width. $200/300

155. Aqua Silk Jacket Dress and Bonnet
Of aqua silk, the princess-style dress with front closure is decorated with box-pleated ivory silk border has attached jacket with hook closure at the center waist. The dress features three variant decorative bands at the skirt including diamond point and pleats, and each is bordered by cream silk trim. There is lace trim at cuffs and along the jacket edges. Included is matching bonnet of richly draped silk with lace and ribbons, wire frame, silk lining. To fit doll about 17". 4" shoulder width. 11" overall length. $400/500

156. Aqua Silk Faille Princess-Style Dress with Batiste Sleeves
Of very finely woven aqua silk faille, the dress features three vertical pleats on either side of front opening whose hook-and-eye closure is disguised by lace ruffle and bronze silk bows with rosette centers. A pleated horizontal band edges the knife-pleated hem with lace-edged muslin underhem. The capelet sleeves and skirt band are bordered by cream cording, and there are lace ruffles and bronze silk bows at the skirt band and rounded neckline. Lace-edged batiste short sleeves are attached to the capelet sleeves. To fit doll about 18". 4" shoulder width. 12" overall length. $300/400

back of dress, #155

157. Printed Cotton Princess Dress with Lace and Silk Trim
A crisp cotton muslin fabric with daintily printed floral design in red, blue and green features princess lines with slight V-neckline edged in cotton lace, front closure, dropped waist with a double row of gathers edged by cotton lace and a hidden border of red silk pleats at the bottom hem. The overlapped edges of the sleevelets are edged with cotton lace, and the dress is fully muslin lined. To fit doll about 23". 6" shoulder width. 15" overall length. $400/500

158. Printed Cotton Dress with Defined Waist
A very delicate abstract floral pattern on cream is featured on this deceptively simple dress with a stitch-defined waist, slight gathers to the upper skirt, banding at the center of the skirt with fuller gathers below, rounded neck with a wide embroidered and cutwork border with scalloped edge, matching trim at short sleeves. A band of medallion patterned cutwork and embroidery extends down the front of the dress and around the bottom hem. The dress has four handmade button holes and buttons at the back. To fit doll about 15". 3" shoulder width. 10" overall length. $200/300

159. Brown Cotton Princess-Style Dress with Feather Stitching
Of cocoa brown cotton printed with tiny rose and cream petals, the dress attains its shape from five vertical bands of stitched-down pleating on either side of the front opening that has two handmade button holes and buttons, and a thread loop and button at the neckline. The sleevelets are gathered at both edges for shape, and the neckline is edged with cream tatting. There are 16 stitched-down vertical tucks at the back, and the skirt is trimmed with red double-cast feather-stitched borders. To fit doll about 21". 5 1/2" shoulder width. 13" overall length. $200/250

160. Very Fine Cotton Princess-Style Dress with Torchon Lace and Silk Faille Trim
The cream cotton fabric is delicately printed with tiny abstract petals that appear to cascade down the length of the princess-styled dress. Three tucks center each side of the button-front dress and end in ruching at the waist; the same pattern is repeated at the back. An ivory silk faille ribbon is attached at the hips, above a 2" border of torchon lace and a pleated underskirt. There is matching lace at the cuffs of the 3/4 sleeves, and red silk cording at the sleeve and neckline edging. The upper dress is lined and there is a small fitted bustle at the back. To fit doll about 23". 6" shoulder width. 14" overall length. $400/500

161. Straw Bonnet with Red Velvet Ribbon
Tightly woven straw bonnet with rounded top, upturned wide brim, wide red velvet folded band with large red velvet bow, cream sateen lining and cord. 2 1/2" inside head width. 5" overall width. $300/400

162. Two-Color Straw Bonnet
Bee-hive shaped straw bonnet in brown and natural straw with lacquered finish, is decorated with tiny red and white flowers. The inside brim is lined with burgundy silk, and the peak of the hat is lined with ivory silk. 2" inside head width. 4" overall width. $300/400

163. Rose Cotton Princess-Style Dress with Cutwork Trim
A dainty neat dress with tapered princess shape of crisp rose cotton, V-shaped front insert of pink and white striped cotton centered by a row of decorative buttons and full-length lapels that hide button closure and are edged by scalloped cutwork. The dress has coat sleeves with wide stitched down cuffs edged with striped fabric and cutwork, and matching collar. There are matching pockets on each side, a 1 1/2" band of vertical pleats at the hemline, and fitted darts at the back waist that give shape to the slightly flared back. To fit doll about 20". 5" shoulder width. 13" overall length. $400/500

164. Rose Striped Cotton Dropped Waist Dress
Finely woven rose cotton with very narrow blue and red striped pattern has dart shaping at front and back, 3/4 coat sleeves with lace-edged cutwork cuffs, rounded collar with wide cutwork border, matching border at the hips, and pleated lower skirt. The dress buttons at the front with seven handmade button holes and pearl buttons. To fit doll about 15". 4" shoulder width. 10" overall length. $200/300

165. Blue Cotton Chambray Jacket Dress
A princess-style dress of striped rose, cream and blue cotton has a blue cotton chambray attached 3/4 jacket with scalloped cutwork edging, tiny pockets, matching coat sleeves with faux-striped cuffs and cutwork edging. The jacket is dart-shaped at the back and lightly tacked onto the pleated striped skirt. The dress buttons at the front with nine handmade buttonholes and tiny pearl buttons. To fit doll about 18". 5" shoulder width. 11" overall length. $300/400

166. Petite White Cotton Dress and Woven Straw Bonnet
Of fine muslin cotton, the dress has a rounded neckline, capelet sleeves, and dropped waist. An open lace insert centers the front panel and is edged by dainty lace with matching lace at sleeves and hips. The neckline is edged with scalloped cutwork, and gathered lace forms the lower skirt; a drawstring petticoat is included. Along with a very fine tightly woven white straw bonnet with cream silk edging and ribbons, floral trim, and stiffened muslin lining. To fit doll about 9". 2 1/2" shoulder width. 5 1/2" overall length. $400/500

167. Patterned Cotton Sateen Two Piece Dress and Bonnet
Of fine cotton sateen with delicately printed floral pattern on cream ground, the ensemble features a waist length fitted jacket with full sleeves tapered at the lace-edged cuffs, rose organza gathered collar, V-shaped tail at the back; draped overskirt above a slightly gathered pin-striped rose/cream underskirt. Included is a silver grey straw bonnet with sunken peak, upturned wide grim, and decorated with rose silk faille ribbons and white organza clusters. To fit doll about 20". 4" shoulder width. 12" overall length. $400/500

168. Rose Velvet Bonnet
Of rich coral rose velvet with flat top, rounded band, and graduated width brim that is very wide at the top. The hat is decorated with soft rose silk satin wide bands and bows and has a flounce of organza at the inside top. White muslin lining and buckram stiffening. 2 3/4" inside width. 6" overall width. $250/300

169. Ivory Satin Two-Piece Gown with Alencon Lace
Of luxurious ivory silk satin, the costume features bodice with V-shape pleated from the banded waist centering a lace-covered panel and lace ruffle, rounded neckline, generously gathered full sleeves with ruffled lace at the bands, hook-and-eye closure at the back. With full-length skirt having gored shaping at the sides, flat front, box-pleats at the back with extended train. The skirt is fully lined for shaping, and has a lace-edged ruffle at the hem. The skirt front is trimmed with wide borders of Alencon lace and silk rosettes. To fit doll about 23". 4" shoulder width. 12" waist. $500/700

170. Ivory Satin High-Waisted Gown with Pouf Sleeves
Of ivory satin, the high-waisted gown features a low-rounded neckline, very full sleeves that achieve their shape from narrow inner lining, flat front full-length skirt that tapers outwards at the sides, box-pleats at the center back with slightly-lengthened back skirt. The gown is decorated by gathered organza over the front and back of the bodice. To fit doll about 24". 6" shoulder width. 19" overall length. $400/500

171. Large Ivory Satin Gown with Extended Train and Bonnet
Of exceptionally luxurious ivory silk satin, the full length gown features a fitted bodice with gathering at the center front and back, constructed waist, gore-shaped skirt with very long train, modified gigot-sleeves with gathered fullness at the shoulders and fitted lower arms. The gown is fully lined, and has additional netting for shape in skirt and train, and is decorated with organza flounces. Along with organza-over-canvas bonnet with ivory silk ribbon curls framing the face. To fit doll about 37". 9" shoulder width. 22" waist. $900/1300

172. Ivory Silk Satin Gown with Extended Train
Of ivory silk satin, the full-length gown features a low-rounded neckline, fitted bodice draped with pleated ivory satin bands, fitted waist, flat-front full skirt (silk frail at waist) that achieves its shape from inset panels at the sides, with narrow box-pleats at the back, elongated train, full sleeves that achieve their shape from narrow pleats at the shoulders and gathered cuffs. The dress is decorated by a wide lace collar overlaid with silk petals, ruffled lace at the sleeves, and a pleated ruffle along the entire hem and train. Fully lined with lace ruffle at skirt bottom. To fit doll about 19". 5" shoulder width. 11" waist. 15" overall. $400/500

173. Rose Silk Wire-Framed Bonnet
A wire-brimmed bonnet is richly covered with three bands of gathered rose silk on the interior brim centered by a lining of cream silk over net stiffening. The outside is also richly covered with gathered silk, white feathers and rose silk streamers. 2" inside head width. 4" overall width. $300/400

174. Petite Ivory Silk Faille Dress
Of ribbed ivory silk faille the dress features a dropped waist with overlaid lace bodice having wide lace bretelles that extend down the back, pleated skirt, 3/4 length sleeves with puffed shoulders and lace edging, rose silk ribbons. With attached slip and pantalets. To fit doll about 11". 2" shoulder width. 7" overall length. $200/300

175. French Black Leather Shoes, Size 8
Of black leather with black overcast stitching, straps with two buttons, black silk rosettes, tan leather undersoles incised with figure of doll in chemise and number "8". 3". $200/250

176. Bronze Green Silk Dress with Juliette Sleeves
Of very lustrous bronze green silk, the dress features a low rounded neckline with gathering at the bodice top and box pleats above the constructed waist at both front and back, hook-and-eye closure at the back, full gathered skirt with muslin lining, Juliette sleeves that are very full at the upper half and snugly fitting the lower arm. The dress is decorated with lace ruffles at the shoulders and a rose silk ribbon. To fit doll about 23". 5" shoulder width. 12" waist. 16" overall length. $500/700

177. Ivory and Patterned Silk Dress with Back Lacing
Ivory silk satin dress with fitted bodice and waist, V-shaped yoke with scalloped edge patterned silk centering an embroidered net panel, V-shaped waist with cording, pleated full skirt with double row of scalloped patterned silk ruffle, straight short sleeves with tulle overlay, nine handmade bone-strengthened lacing holes with original laces, lined bodice. To fit doll 22". 5" shoulder width. 12" waist. 15" overall length. $400/500

178. Rose Silk Gown with Juliette Sleeves
Of softest pale rose silk with delicately shaded floral design in darker rose color, the high-waisted dress features bodice with center V-shaped pleats, constructed waist, rounded neckline, Juliette sleeves that are very full at the upper half and snugly fitting the lower arm (constructed with gathers at underseams), gathered waist of long skirt, eight tiny pearl buttons and button holes at the back. The dress is trimmed with rose silk satin pleats at the neckline and around the

hem, and has matching draped waist sash with rosette center; the skirt is lined in ivory silk faille with pink silk scalloped dust ruffle. To fit doll about 24". 5" shoulder width. 13" waist. 18" overall length. $600/800

179. Four Bebe Stays for Bebe Jumeau
Of blue or cream cotton sateen with ribbed shaping, lace edging, and brass-edged lacing grommets, and original laces. 6", 9", 12" and 14" waists. $300/400

180. White Cotton Petticoat and Pantalets
Of crisp white cotton, the set features pantalets with drawstring waist, fitted leg band above a cutwork ruffle; and with matching petticoat with tie-back structured waistband above a cutwork ruffle above the hem. 16" waist. $200/300

181. Lavender Silk Dress for Size 12 Bebe Jumeau
Of soft lavender silk satin padded overall for luxurious effect, the dress features a fitted bodice with alternate 1" bands of ruched fabric and embroidered lace at both front and back, fitted ruched neckline, long sleeves with lace cuffs and lace bretelles, band of ruching just below the waist opens into full gathered skirt that is trimmed with a 3" band of lace at the hem. Hook-and-eye closure, silk shoulder bows. 6" shoulder width. 14" waist. 16" overall length. $500/700

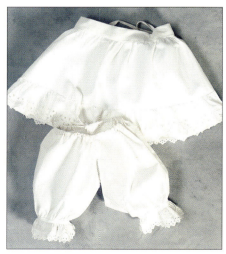

182. Large Rose Silk Faille Dress and Ivory Faille Bonnet
Of finest rose silk faille, with square cut neckline edged in thick cotton lace, loose pleated front with wide inverted pleat at the center, very full poufy sleeves that achieve their shape from straight-cut sleeve lining and fitted 1" arm band also trimmed with cotton lace. Four rose silk ribbon rosettes decorate the bodice and there is rose featherstitching along the hem. Along with ivory silk faille bonnet with pleated medallion back, three tiers of ruffles, box pleated face ruffle with organza lining, padded silk lining. To fit doll about 30". 8" shoulder width. 20" overall length. $500/700

183. Rose Silk Dress and Undergarments for Bebe Jumeau, Size 10
Of soft rose silk satin with gathered full bodice overlaid with ruffled Bertha collar, very full sleeves with fitted bands to allow pouf to be dramatically displayed (sleeve silk worn), pleated full skirt with inverted box pleat at center, lined bodice, hook-and-eye closure, feather-stitching at collar and hem. Along with Jumeau white cotton slip and pantalets with matching cutwork trim. To fit Bebe Jumeau, size 10. 6 1/2" shoulder width. 14" waist. 15" overall length. $400/500

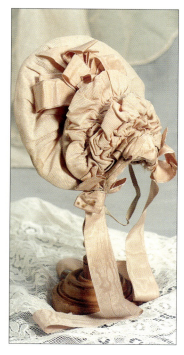

184. Rose Silk Faille Bonnet
The wire-framed bonnet of rose silk faille features an elaborately ruched bonnet back trimmed with rose silk ribbons and streamers, with graduated width brim, padded net lining. 3" inside head with. 5" overall diameter. $300/400

185. Petite Textured Rose Silk Dress
Of rose silk with unusual textured floral design, the tiny dress features box pleats from the rounded neckline, lace sleevelets, ruffled lace collar and hemline trim, rose silk ribbons. Along with muslin lace-edged handkerchief with rose silk ribbons, and wire-framed lace bonnet with rose silk ribbons. To fit doll about 7". $400/500

186. Peach Silk Dress for Bebe Jumeau, Size 7
Of fine peach silk satin, the dropped waist dress features gathered yoke between bretelles, lace edged rounded collar, very full sleeves with gathering at the shoulders and lace-lined edges, wide waistband of floral-woven peach silk that extends to the hips, gathered skirt with embroidered lace overskirt, muslin pleated dust ruffle. Included are four pieces of matching undergarments, two with peach silk ribbon trim. For Bebe Jumeau, size 7, original Jumeau costume. $1200/1500

187. Rose Silk High-Waisted Dress
Of luxurious rose silk satin the high-waisted dress features a fitted bodice with gathered full skirt, lace-edged neckline, 3/4 length sleeves with fitted lace-edged cuffs, lace-edged hem, hook and loop closure, full lining. To fit doll about 22". 5" shoulder width. 15" overall length. $400/500

188. Magenta Silk Bonnet with Ivory Silk Ribbons
The flat-back bonnet with wire frame is fronted by a generous graduated width brim with ruffled detail. The front of the bonnet is centered by a magenta silk medallion with ivory silk bow and streamers that extend to the back of the bonnet, forming a large bow. Ruched organza edges the face, and the bonnet has white silk lining. 3" head width. 7" overall width. $300/400

189. Magenta Velvet and Lace Bonnet
Rich magenta velvet bonnet with gathered back, graduated width brim with pleated construction on the underside and detailed lace overlay on the back. With wire frame and stiffening buckram. 2 1/2" inside head width. 8"h. $200/300

190. White Fur Muff and Collar in Store Box
The lush white fur muff with ermine tips, red silk bow, ivory silk lining, ivory braided cord is presented in its original box along with matching collar. The box has decorative lithograph on the lid. 4" wide muff. $400/500

191. Red/Cream Striped Cotton Dress for Petite Doll
Of narrow bands of red stripes against wider bands of cream, the cotton high waisted dress has wide Bertha collar, gathered neckline, red silk button trim, short puffed sleeves, hook-and-eye closure, red silk bow. To fit about 8" dolls. 2" shoulder width. 5" overall length. $300/400

192. Brown Leather Bebe Shoes with Red Stockings
Of brown leather with reddish brown overcast stitching, ankle straps with pearl buttons, red silk bows, leather soles incised with hot air balloon and "Marque Depose" and "3". 3 3/4"l. $300/400

193. Two-Color Straw Beehive Bonnet
Two color grey/natural straw bonnet in beehive shape with upturned side brim, lavishly trimmed with red silk banding and ribbons. 3" inside head width. $200/300

194. Red Silk Faille Bonnet and Parasol
Very elaborate red silk faille bonnet with full gathered back centered by ruched border panel, and very full graduated width wire-framed front ruffle with red silk bow and feather trim, cotton sateen lining. Along with red cotton sateen parasol with lace and red silk ribbon edging, white wooden handle with brown sculpted dog head handle. 5" inside head width. 10"h bonnet. 17"l parasol. $400/500

**195. Ivory Silk Satin Dress
with Velvet Bonnet and Silk Parasol**
Luxurious ivory silk satin high-waisted dress with fitted yoke, full gathered skirt, very full puffed sleeves. The dress is fully lined and has an unusually designed lace decoration at the bodice with matching trim at the sleeve bands and two rows of lace at the hem. Included is a velvet bonnet with flat top, graduated width brim with decorative ribbon and feather, and an ivory silk parasol with lace edging, wooden handle with gilded hand grip and tip, silk ribbons. To fit doll about 22". 6" shoulder width. 15" overall length. $600/800

196. Ivory Silk Satin Dress with Matching Silk Bonnet
Of very luxurious ivory silk satin, the high-waisted dress features fitted yoke trimmed with alternate bands of border and inset lace, full gathers dropping from the yoke, very full sleeves fitted from the elbow to wrist with lace cuffs, button and loop closure. And ivory silk satin bonnet with triple rows of ruching at the back easing into very full gathers with box-pleated bavolet. The bonnet has a wide silk ruffle framing the face backed by diamond point edged lace and fronted by sheer organza, net lining, streamers. To fit doll about 20". 5 1/2" shoulder width. 14" overall length. $500/700

197. Ivory Satin Bonnet with Milliner's Label
The ivory satin wire framed bonnet is designed with gathering at the sides, allowing the brim to be turned up (as shown) or worn low over the head in more traditional coiffe style. The bonnet is decorated with delicate flowers, has silk lining, and gilt lettered milliner's label. 3" inside head width. 4" overall diameter. $200/300

198. Ivory Silk Satin Bonnet with Bavolet
Wire framed bonnet of fine ivory silk satin is richly gathered at the back and framed by a wide band of ruffles. The front features a graduated width brim, 4" at its widest point with wire frame to give tightness to the gathering. The bonnet is lined with cream silk and stiffened net, and there is a gathered silk bavolet at the back of the neck. Very narrow silk ribbons form bouquets around the crown. 3 1/2" inside head width. $250/350

199. Black Leather Shoes for E.J. Bebe, Size 5
Of black leather with brown overcast stitching, ankle straps, silver buttons, brown silk rosettes, leather soles incised "E.J. (in circle) Depose 5". 2"l. $200/300

200. Tan Leather Shoes for Bebe Jumeau, Size 11
Of tan leather with ivory overcast stitching, ankle straps with silver buttons, bronze silk bows, leather soles marked with incised full figure of doll, and "11" and "Depose". 4"l. $300/400

201. Purple Silk Blouse and Ivory Silk Bonnet
Of soft purple silk twill, the blouse features an ivory silk faille plastron with gathered shape and fitted neck, very full sleeves with lining for shape, lace-edged cuffs, hook-and-eye closure. Along with an ivory silk satin bonnet with very full ruffled back, double ruffled front, patterned silk band and streamers, padded lining. To fit doll about 21". 5" shoulder width. $400/500

202. Aqua Cotton Twill Dress with Lace Trim
Of sateen finished cotton twill the pretty dress features a constructed waist, box-pleated bodice, short puffed sleeves with lace-overlay bands, pleated skirt with double row of lace edging. There is a lace sash and aqua silk front and back bows, two button and loop closures at the back, lined bodice. To fit doll about 12". 2 1/2" shoulder width. 7" overall length. $200/300

203. Petite Aqua Silk Dress
Of aqua silk satin, the high-waisted dress features V-shaped front and back yoke centered by wide self-bretelles decorated with tucking and having wide heavy cotton lace underlay. The dress has short poufy sleeves with featherstitching at the bands, and the full skirt has gathered hem band with three rows of tucking, featherstitch embroidery and cotton lace peeking out at bottom. To fit doll about 9". 2 1/4" shoulder width. 6" overall length. $400/500

204. Blue Sateen Wire-Framed Bonnet
Rich gathers form the cap of the blue sateen bonnet with stiffened buckram brim wrapped with blue silk ribbons, wire frame with gathers and wide ruffle, ivory silk ribbon trim, tulle lining. 3" inside head width. 10" overall diameter. $300/400

205. Unusual Woven Silk/Twill Bonnet and Aqua Leather Shoes
Of muslin twill like fabric interwoven with stripes of aqua silk, the wire-framed bonnet is designed to sit against the back of head, with wide sunshade framing the face. The fabric is on both the inside and outside of the bonnet and is trimmed with aqua silk faille ribbons and bows, pale blue flower and buckram lining. Along with aqua kid leather shoes with ankle straps, blue rosettes. 3" inside head width. 2 1/4" shoe length. $400/500

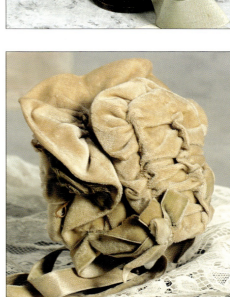

206. Apple Green Silk Twill Dropped Waist Dress
Ribbed green silk twill dress with dropped waist, double set of inverted box pleats at front and back, pleated skirts, wide apple green silk satin hip sash with bow, short cap sleeves, wide cotton-lace collar with diamond points. To fit doll about 12". 3 1/2" shoulder width. 7" overall length. $300/400

207. Aqua Silk Bonnet with Lace Overlay
The aqua silk bonnet is richly padded and gathered to sit against the back of head, decorated with lace overlay, having wire-framed gathered brim that frames the face and is lined on the interior as well as exterior, ivory silk lining. 2" inside head width. 5" overall diameter. $300/400

208. Green Velvet Bonnet
Of thick moss green velvet, the bonnet is designed to sit against the back of head and frame the face, with richly draped velvet at the back framed by a self-ruffle and self-band, and a wire framed front with draped gathering of velvet within a larger velvet ruffle. The bonnet is lined with pale green cotton sateen and has dark green bow and petal trim, green velvet streamers. 3" inside width. 5" overall width. $300/400

209. Cream Velvet Plush Bonnet
Very thick plush velvet forms a bonnet with gathered back centered by silk pom-pom button, graduated width gathered brim, aqua silk draped band with large bow, muslin lining. 3 1/2" inside width. 7" overall diameter. $200/300

210. Pale Green Knit Woolen Dress with Green Silk Bonnet
Intricately knit green woolen princess-style dress with six white woolen scalloped designs at the hem, along with vertical white woolen bands at the front, and a fitted neckline with scalloped designs. The pattern is repeated at the back with scalloped edge opening, pearl buttons with hidden cotton placket having handmade button holes, back pleat with ivory silk bow, full length sleeves with ivory silk wrist bands. Along with green silk wire framed bonnet with elaborate ruching and gathers, feathered boa, stiffened net lining. To fit doll about 22". 6" shoulder width. 14" overall length. $300/400

211. Pale Green Silk Satin Dress and Silk Bonnet
The dropped waist dress features a high fitted yoke hidden under a wide ruffled lace collar, center stitched down pleats, short poufy sleeves with wide lace-overlaid cuffs, widely pleated skirt with lower gathered silk ruffle overlaid with lace, white sheer silk hip sash. The dress is unusually lined with white pique and has hook-and-eye closure. With wire-framed white sheer silk bonnet, richly gathered and decorated with tiny flowers. To fit doll about 18". 3 1/2" shoulder width. 13" overall length. $300/400

212. Ivory Silk Satin Coat and Lace Bonnet
Of luxurious silk satin, the coat features an open front, fitted bodice, and very large cape collar with yellow silk ribbon edging and featherstitching, full-length sleeves with fitted cuffs with ribbons edging and featherstitching, silk ribbon streamers at the front. Along with embroidered tulle cap with pleated lace ruffle over stiffened pleated net, with narrow silk ribbon frou-frou. To fit doll about 20". 6" shoulder width. 13" overall length. $400/500

213. Ivory Silk Satin and Lace Dress with Train
The ivory satin dress has lace-overlay on the entire front panel, open front with hook-and-eye closure trimmed with silk ribbons, ivory silk satin full sleeves with box-pleating at the arm bands, lace overlaid fitted back bodice, ivory satin box pleated back with extended train and 3" lace border on the inside hem of the train. To fit doll about 17". 4" shoulder width. 12" overall front length. 19" overall back length. $300/400

214. Red Woolen Plaid Dress for Bebe Jumeau
Of red and midnight green elaborate woolen plaid, the dress features a fitted bodice with V-shaped pleats below a maroon velvet yoke edged with woolen ruffles, fitted neckline, full sleeves fitted below the elbow with maroon velvet band, self-cording at the waistband, flat-front skirt with gathered back, lace-edged dust ruffle. To fit doll about 20". 4" shoulder width. 10" waist. 13" overall length. $300/400

215. Brown Woolen and Velvet Dress
Of patterned brown wool, the dress features a gathered bodice with fitted velvet yoke, inset 1" waist band, gathered skirt below cartridge pleating, very full upper sleeves that achieve their shape from fitted shape below the elbow, fully lined bodice, hook-and-eye closure. To fit doll about 25". 5" shoulder width. 11" waist. 17" overall length. $300/400

216. Leather Shoes for Bebe Jumeau, Size 11
Of iridescent black leather with brown overcast edging, ankle straps, brown silk rosettes, brown leather soles impressed "Paris Depose" with symbol of bee and "11". 3 1/2"l. $300/400

217. Leather Shoes for Bebe Jumeau, Size 12
Of iridescent black leather with brown overcast edging, ankle straps, brown silk bows, brown leather soles impressed "Paris Depose" with symbol of bee and "12". 4 1/4"l. $250/350

218. Scottish Plaid Woolen Tam
Of fine Scottish wool in red, green and brown plaid, red silk banding around the brim with red silk bow, ivory silk lining with gold printed number "64" on interior lid. Inside brim width 3". Overall width 7". $200/250

219. Brown Textured Wool and Velvet Dress with Drop Waist
Of tiny-block-textured brown wool with ruching at the shoulders and center waist, inset brown velvet V-shaped yoke with gold embroidery edge above a row of four decorative gold buttons, brown velvet collar, long sleeves that are fitted in the front and have three sewn-down pleats that give fullness to the back, dropped waist above two wide tiers of ruffles, lace edging at throat and cuffs, and velvet hip sash. The dress-back features three constructed pleats on either side of hook-and-eye closure, and the dress is fully lined. To fit doll about 28". 8" shoulder width. 22" hips. 17" overall length. $500/700

220. Eleven Pairs of Socks for Bebe Jumeau
White socks, in three variations of patterns as found on Bebes Jumeau, in a variety of colors including brown, tan, cream, black, rust, and white. To fit various sizes. $400/500

221. Cream Woolen Dress with Bronze Green Velvet Trim and Matching Velvet Bonnet
Of fine cream wool, the dress features full gathers dropping from a high fitted bodice with overcast scalloped edging at front and back, very full sleeves that achieve their shape from box-pleats at shoulders and fitted green velvet cuffs, scalloped edging at hem, green velvet banding at fitted neckline, hips and front of dress, button and loop closure. With matching green velvet bonnet with draped wide brim overlaid with a double row of box-pleated nett, and decorated with a large bronze green silk bow. $400/500

222. Cream Velvet Dress
Of lustrous cream velvet with textured vertical ribbing, the dress features a fitted yoke above a generously gathered bodice, fitted waist, full gathered skirt with tight cartridge pleats at the waist, long sleeves that are very full at the shoulders and taper to fit the arm below the elbow, hook-and-eye closure, lined bodice. To fit doll about 21". 4" shoulder width. 12" waist. 14" overall length. $300/400

223. White Fur Collar and Muff in Original Box
Of luxurious white fur with ermine tips and green silk bows, the collar and cuff are lined with padded ivory silk, pale green cord attaches to the muff. The set is preserved in its original gift box with gold embossing and design of woman in green flowered hat on its lid. For doll about 18"–22". $300/400

224. Burgundy Flannel and Velvet Dress
Of burgundy flannel lightweight wool, the dress features a high fitted yoke at front and back with full gathered skirt below, very full sleeves with fitted wide cuffs. The dress is trimmed with burgundy velvet collar with cascading diamond-point velvet ribbons to the edge of the yoke, black velvet banding on sleeves, and has full lining and hook-and-eye closure. To fit doll about 20". 4 1/2" shoulder width. 14" overall length. $200/300

225. Pale Yellow Cashmere Wool Flowered Dress
Of finest delicate cashmere wool in palest yellow color printed with delicate rose petals, the dress features vertically tucked bodice set above a fitted waist with self cording, full gathered skirt, very full sleeves with 2 1/2" fitted cuffs, lace bretelles and lace edging at neckline, double-stitched blue feathering at hem, cuffs and bodice. To fit doll about 20", 3 1/2" shoulder width. 12" waist. 14" overall length. $400/500

226. Magenta Silk Shoes
Of luxurious magenta silk with light brown overcast edging, magenta pom-poms, ankle straps, and brown leather soles impressed "10" and "Made in Germany". 3 1/2"l. $300/400

227. Complete Communion Ensemble for Bebe Jumeau, Size 8, in Samaritaine Box
The ensemble comprises sheer batiste dress with vertical pleats on bodice, five bands of tucking on skirt, full sleeves fitted down elbows down and decorated with five bands of tucks, fitted waist with ivory sash, button and loop closure. Along with undergarments comprising full slip and petticoat. With long veil, flowered coronet, candle, silk ribbons, crystal bead necklace and bracelet, gold plated brooch, rosary with coral beads, batiste reticule with lace-edged handkerchief, white kid leggings, white kid shoes inscribed "8", and a blue leather bound missal. Included is a French handwritten note detailing the contents and original box with Samaritaine Paris department store in which the ensemble has been stored. 6" shoulder width. 5" waist. 15" overall length. $700/900

228. Trousseau for Bebe Jumeau, Size 11
The trousseau comprises red and white striped school-dress with red silk ribbon trim and "11" label; plaid flannel woolen coat with hood, brass buttons, red silk lining and "11" label; blue striped party skirt with lace trim and white silk blouse; black and brown checkered raincoat with hood; burgundy velvet coat with middy collar, black silk appliqué, gold buttons, muslin lining, original "11" label; matching burgundy velvet bonnet with rose silk petals; two nightshirts, pantalets, combination and two petticoats. $1200/1500

Chapter IV: *Sailor Dresses*

229. Blue Cotton Middy Dress in Original Box
Blue cotton sleeveless sailor dress with yellow pencil stripes, has lace-edged neckline and embroidered yellow anchor on bodice, under navy blue long-sleeved hip-length jacket with striped middy collar and cuffs. The jacket has pearl buttons down the front, and is presented in its original box with gilt metal long-handled net, in original box with lithograph of children at the seashore on its lid. To fit doll about 24". 6" shoulder width. 15" overall length. $600/800

**230. Tan Leather Sailor Hat "Mignon"
for Louvre Department Store**
Of tan leather with firm-sided banding having brown grosgrain silk ribbon labeled "Mignon" in gilt lettering, silk twill lining with gold stamp of Grand Magasins du Louvre. 4 1/2" inside head width. $200/300

232. Brown Leather Sailor Hat "Regatta"
Of reddish-brown leather with firm-sided banding, having black grosgrain silk ribbon labeled "Regatta" in gilt lettering, gold

cotton sateen lining. 6" inside head width. $200/300

233. Blue Cotton Sailor Dress with Blouson Bodice
Of crisp homespun-like blue cotton, the dress features a dropped waist styling with blouson bodice, detachable yoke with ten white bands and stand-up cutwork collar, wide middy collar with white banding, long sleeves with turned-up banded cuffs, skirt with box-pleated all around and white bands at the hemline. To fit slim-bodied doll about 23". 5" shoulder width. 15" overall length. $500/700

234. Navy Blue Woolen Sailor Cap with Gilt Aviation Stamp
The navy blue woolen sailor cap with navy blue grosgrain ribbon banding has an additional blue silk ribbon across the top with gilt-stamped design of Wright Brothers airplane. 4" inside head width. $100/200

235. Petite Navy Blue Middy Jacket
Of navy blue wool the jacket features brass buttons on either side of front-opening jacket, middy collar with white banding, gathered shoulders with flaps at wrists, blue cotton sateen lining. To fit doll about 12". 3" shoulder width. 4" length. $200/300

236. Large Navy Blue Sailor Costume
from Old England Store in Paris
Of heavy navy blue wool the two-piece sailor costume comprises jacket with hidden buttons at front closure, wool middy collar with detachable dark blue cotton over-collar trimmed with three bands of white braid, long sleeves with sewn-down darts at the wrists, breast pocket, silk tie. With fully-lined matching long pants having fly-front with lacing closure and back button flap. The jacket has silk label "Old England, Paris". To fit doll about 35". 12" shoulder width. 20" waist. $600/800

237. White Pique and Blue Sateen
Boy's Sailor Ensemble for Bebe Jumeau, Size 11
Three-piece ensemble features a white pique short jacket with box pleats at the front and back, very wide full sleeves with shoulder gathering, blue rounded cotton sateen collar and matching tie and turned up cuffs, each trimmed with three rows of white banding. Along with navy blue cotton sateen short pants with button fly-front and silver buttons on legs, and blue cotton sateen sailor cap with lighter blue band trimmed with white banding. The jacket has label "11" inside jacket. To fit Bebe Jumeau, size 11. 6 1/2" shoulder width. 16" waist. $500/700

238. Navy Blue Wool and Blue
Chambray Sailor Ensemble
The two-piece ensemble features sleeveless dress with dropped waist bodice of blue chambray over pleated skirt; along with blue woolen hip-length jacket with chambray middy collar. The bodice and collar are trimmed with three bands of white piping. There are brass buttons on jacket and dart-shaping on sleeves. To fit doll about 16". 4" shoulder width. 11" overall length. $300/400

239. Navy Blue Wool and Blue Chambray Sailor Ensemble for Bebe Jumeau, Size 11
The two-piece ensemble features sleeveless dress with dropped waist bodice of blue chambray over pleated skirt; along with blue woolen hip-length jacket with chambray middy collar. The bodice and collar are trimmed with five bands of white piping. There are brass buttons on jacket and dart-shaping on sleeves. Original "11" label on jacket. To fit size 11 Jumeau bebe. 24" doll. 6" shoulders. 16" overall. $500/700

240. Navy Blue Wool Sailor Cap "Paris"
Of navy blue wool with wire frame shaping, the sailor cap has black grosgrain band labeled "Paris", streamers, pale blue cotton lining. 4 1/2" inside head width. $200/300

100

241. Cream and Navy Blue Sailor Ensemble
Of cream and navy blue wool, the ensemble features a cream flannel blouse with button front, short sleeves with navy blue banding, V-shaped rolled collar with white wool edging; with blue pleated wool skirt having button attachment to blouse at front and back, blue embroidered anchor on blouse. To fit doll about 22". 5" shoulder width. 12" overall length. $400/500

242. Navy Blue Knit Sailor Set for Bebe Jumeau, Size 8
Of fine navy blue woolen knit, the set comprises sweater with striped middy collar and yoke, short sleeves with white knit detailing, ribbed waistband, along with matching short pants. With matching knit cap with stiff navy blue band trimmed with white silk grosgrain band and silk pom-pom. The hat is labeled "8". To fit doll about 20". 5" shoulder width. $400/500

243. White Pique Sailor Dress with Blue Chambray Accents
The two-piece ensemble features a sleeveless dress with dropped waist bodice of blue chambray centering muslin sides and back, above a pleated skirt with wide box-pleated front panel. With hip-length jacket featuring blue chambray collar edged in white piping, and long sleeves with gathering at the shoulders and blue chambray cuffs with white piping, four decorative buttons. To fit doll about 20". 5" shoulder width. 13" overall length. $400/500

244. Red and White Sailor Costume with Red Hat
The ensemble features a sleeveless dress with bodice of red flannel centered by rose cotton, constructed waist, skirt with flat-front panel and wide box pleats. With white cashmere sailor jacket with large middy collar and short sleeves with wide cuffs, red bow tie. Along with pressed red felt flannel flat-top hat with very wide flat brim and red silk band and ties. To fit doll about 22". 7" shoulder width. 12" overall length. $400/500

245. Navy Blue Wool Sailor Ensemble with Sailor Hat from Au Nain Bleu
The three-piece navy blue wool ensemble features a sleeveless dress with white shadowpane cotton bodice above a pleated blue woolen skirt; along with navy blue jacket having white pique middy collar and turn-up cuffs with inset bands of embroidery. Along with navy blue sailor cap with blue silk band labeled "Lutin" in gilt lettering, muslin lining with original Au Nain Bleu label on interior. To fit doll about 22". 6" shoulder width. 13" overall length. $600/800

246. Navy Blue Flannel Sailor Costume
Comprising sleeveless dress with navy blue cotton twill front panel centered by muslin sides and back, constructed waist, pleated skirt. With hip-length sailor style jacket with middy collar trimmed with three white bands, long sleeves with pleated fullness at the shoulders and sewn-down darts at the wrists, hook-and-eye closure, three decorative brass buttons. To fit doll about 23". 6" shoulder width. 13" waist. 14" overall length. $400/500

247. Three-Piece Black Velvet and Wool Sailor Ensemble
Comprising a black velvet jacket with self-banded rounded collar, double-breasted construction with hook-and-eye closure and decorative brass buttons, long sleeves with gathers at the shoulders and sewn-down carts at the wrist end, flaps on faux-pockets, ivory silk twill lined with blue overcast stitching. Along with navy blue wool box-pleated skirt with set-in waist band and two bands of white trim. With matching black velvet sailor cap trimmed with white bands and lined. The jacket has label with initial "F". To fit doll about 20". 6" shoulder width. 12" waist. $500/700

248. Red Lightweight Woolen Sailor Dress
Of dark red wool in very lightweight texture, the sailor dress has dropped waist, fitted yoke hidden under very wide V-shaped collar that extends entirely around the back, rounded neckline, box pleats below the yoke forming blouson bodice, box pleats below the hips, elbow length very full sleeves with constructed bands. The dress is trimmed with narrow bands of black velvet ribbon centered by white appliqué flowers and lace, and has red silk sash with large bow at the back, hook-and-eye closure, fully lined bodice. To fit doll about 18". 5" shoulder width. 11" overall length. $400/500

249. Red and White Cotton Sailor Costume
Of red and white checkered fine cotton flannel, the set comprises sleeveless dress with checkered front panel centering a white pique stripe, muslin sides and back, constructed waist with red and white pleats all-around. With matching jacket having white pique middy collar with diamond point shaping at front, white cording and plaid border, very full long sleeves with sewn-down pleats at wrists. To fit doll about 22". 6" shoulder width. 15" waist. 13" overall length. $400/500

250. Red Cashmere Wool Sailor Style Costume
Of dark red cashmere wool (some moth holes) the costume comprises fitted jacket with dart-shaped fitting being short in the back and extending to points at the front waist, with inset plastron that closes with hooks and eyes at the center and is trimmed with ivory braid; coat sleeves with gathered shaping along the underseam, hook-and-eye closures at wrists with three bands of ivory trim. Matching full skirt with wide waistband trimmed with white banding and rosette at side waist, cartridge pleating, and with six rows of ivory trim around the skirt center and hem. With matching sailor style cap having fullness at the banding that is trimmed with ivory braid and rosette. To fit doll about 22". 4" shoulder width 10" waist. $500/700

251. Red Knit Middy Shirt with Red Velvet Pants and Woolen Cap for Bebe Jumeau, Size 12
The red knit short-sleeved middy blouse has white grosgrain ribbon edging on collar, and red and white striped knit V-shaped insert. With belted red velvet short pants with button fly-front and gold decorative buttons on side leg seams. And with red woolen sailor's cap with red grosgrain banding labeled "Jean Bart" in gold. The middy shirt (some moth holes) has original Jumeau size label "8". To fit doll about 20". 5" shoulder width. 13" waist. $500/700

252. Two Maroon Woolen Sailor Dresses
Of maroon wool, the dresses each feature dropped waist design with box-pleated skirts, wide sashes, lace-edged necklines and middy shaped collars. One has low V-shaped collar centering nine cream stripes, with long sleeves and four white stripes around the hemline, to fit 17" doll, 4" shoulder width, 12" overall length. The other has five stripes inside the more modest collar, shorter sleeves, two bands of cream trim around the skirt. To fit 16" doll. 3 1/2" shoulder width. 11" overall length. $600/800

253. Tan Leather Boots and Sailor Hat, Belt and Leggings
Comprising sailor hat of tan leather with brown grosgrain ribbon banding and streamers, labeled "Mignon" in gilt letters, silk twill lining, and tan leather boots with brass-grommet lacing holes and overcast edging, marked "8" (indicating size 8 Bebe Jumeau); and white leather belt with four adjustable holes; and brown knit leggings with white foot straps. To fit Bebe Jumeau, size 8. 3" shoe length. 4" inside head width. $400/600

254. Brown/Cream Striped Sailor Dress in Original Box
Of brown and cream stripes in cotton serge, the one-piece dress features a wide V-shaped detachable collar that extends into a large square collar at the back, with very full sleeves gathered at the shoulders with sewn-down pleats around the wrists, full-length box pleats extending from the shoulders, leatherette brown belt, belt loops, muslin lining, brass "Bebe" pin. The dress is presented in its original store box with decorative papers. To fit doll about 22". 5 1/2" shoulder width. 15" overall length. $600/800

255. Rose Silk Middy Dress and Jacket with Gilt Anchors
Of rose silk or fine sateen with interwoven rose striping, the sleeveless dress features box-pleated bodice with self-banded neckline, set-in waist, box-pleated front skirt with wide gored panels at the sides and gathered skirt at the back. With short matching middy jacket having rose-silk edged lapels with cotton lace, Juliette sleeves with gathered fullness at the shoulders and fitted below the elbows, the lower sleeves are lace covered and the dress is decorated with rose silk ribbons, gilt anchors, and rows of rose silk covered buttons down the sides and around the hem. Along with original muslin petticoat and white cotton cutwork petticoat. To fit doll about 20". 5" shoulder width. 12" waist. 14" overall length. $900/1200

Chapter V:
Jackets, Coats and Outerwear

256. Midnight-Blue Velvet Coat
Of luxurious velvet in darkest midnight blue, the coat features V-shaped neck with wide rounded and tapered collar edged in silk, shaped coat sleeves. The coat is lined in textured aqua silk that also forms the underside of the collar. To fit doll about 22". 6" shoulder width. 14" overall length. $300/400

257. Midnight-Blue Velvet Coat for Bebe Jumeau, Size 8
Of very rich dark blue velvet, the coat features flared sides, brass button and loop closure, middy-style collar tapered at the front and box-shaped at the back, coat sleeves, white cotton lining. The cuffs and collar are trimmed with black braid. An original cloth Jumeau size label "8" appears at back of collar. 5 1/2" shoulder width. 12" overall length. $200/300

257A. Navy Blue Wool Jacket
Of fine navy blue wool, the neatly shaped jacket features high-cut V-shaped neckline, four brass button closure, flared sides, very full gathered sleeves with constructed cuffs having sewn-down flaps, overcast stitch trim, two back hip flaps for fit, silk lining of very narrowly striped silk. To fit doll about 22". 5" shoulder width. 11" overall length. $200/300

258. Navy Blue Wool Double-Breasted Coat
Of thick navy blue wool, the double-breasted coat features two rows of brass buttons, lapel collar rounded at the back, coat sleeves with brass button trim, faux-pocket flaps, hip belt, silk lining. An original cloth Jumeau size label "8" appears at back of collar. 6" shoulder width. 12" overall length. $200/300

259. Black Woolen Uniform Jacket and Cap
Of fine black wool, the double-breasted jacket features lapel collar formed of wool at the front lapels and black velvet at the rounded back, two rows of brass buttons, long sleeves with brass buttons, striped sateen lining. Along with black woolen cap with firm leather brim and band, gold braid and embroidered leaf medallion. To fit slim-bodied doll abut 18". 4" shoulder width. 3 1/4" inside head width. $400/500

260. Light Brown Woolen Coat and Lambswool Collar
Very fine quality light brown woolen coat fitted at the top with flared sides for shape, has deeply notched lapel collar, coat sleeves with unusual darts at the shoulders, three button front, and decorative overcast dark brown stitching at all edges, ivory sateen lining. Along with curly lambswool collar with bear's head and tail trim, silk chain closure. To fit doll about 22". 5" shoulder width. 15" overall length. $400/500

261. Light Brown Woolen Jacket
Very fine quality light brown woolen jacket with rounded cape collar below a smaller rounded collar that terminates in long front flaps for tying at the throat, flared sides, tiny metal buttons, coat sleeves with rich gathers at the fitted cuff bands, fully lined. To fit doll about 18". 4 1/2" shoulder width. 9" length. $200/250

262. Taupe Flannel Wool Coat with Red Wool Trim and Red Beret
Of lightweight soft flannel wool the flared-side coat features wide cape collar that extends around the back, coat sleeves with fullness at the shaped cuffs, silk lining, silver-edged red velvet trim at collar and cuffs, tiny brass buttons. Along with matching red woolen beret with silk pom-pom. The set is presented in its original gift box with engraving of children on the lid. To fit about 18" doll. 6" shoulder width. 10" overall length. 3" inside hat width. 7" overall head width. $600/800

263. Collection of Salesman's Sample Caps with Original Labels
Seventeen doll-sized caps for men and boy's in various styles, colors and fabrics, with professional quality construction details including leather inside bands, lining, darts and shaping. The styles include military, uniform, golfing, jockey, and others. The military caps are labeled as to unit and region. Included are the caps shown here, with original hand-lettered labels for each. To fit dolls about 18". 3 1/2"–4" inside head width. $1500/2000

264. Flannel Wool Plaid Hooded Coat for Bebe Jumeau, Size 11 or 12
Of rich flannel wool, the Scottish plaid coat features flat front with flared sides, full gathered hood whose neck shape can appear as collar points when the hood is worn down, full pleated long sleeves with overcast edging at cuffs, hook-and-eye closure with two series of decorative brass buttons at the front and a back hip sash with brass buttons. The coat is fully lined with red sateen, and has Jumeau size label in the neck (11 or 12). To fit doll about 24"–26". 7" shoulder width. 16" overall length, excluding hood. $400/500

265. Red Woolen Jacket with Au Louvre-Labeled Scottish Tam
The jacket features flat front and back with tapered sides, wide collar beneath a smaller collar overlaid with lace that extends inside the jacket, very full sleeves with wide fitted ivory silk and lace cuffs that match the ivory silk jacket lining. With matching red woolen tam with Scottish plaid binding, red feather and silver medallion; lined with red silk that has gilt lettering "Louvre" and reclining lion, indicating a specialty item from the Paris department store Au Louvre. To fit doll about 24". 7" shoulder width. 10" length. $400/500

266. Fancy Red Silk and Black Leather Boots
Of red silk with canvas lining, the high boots feature black leather tips, lacing inserts and leg bands, brass grommeted lacing holes, soft kid soles with darker leather edges in the manner of signed Huret shoes. 4 1/2"l. $200/300

267. Light Brown Cord-du-Roi Coat and Hat
Of light brown velvety corduroy (*cord-du-roi*) the flat front coat features very wide flare at the sides, waist-length rounded collar edged with lace, very full 3/4 sleeves with fitted cuffs, ivory sateen lining. With matching hat having flat top, wide band with upturned brim, decorated with draped light brown silk ribbons, silk and net lining. To fit doll about 16". 3 1/2" shoulder width. 10" overall length. 2 1/2" inside cap width. $200/300

268. Red/Cream Shadowpane Jacket with Lapels
Of woven wool/linen in checkered shadowpane design of red and cream, the flat-front jacket features slightly flared sides, and very full sleeves with fitted red sateen cuffs, red sateen shaped lapels at the front that evolve into rounded shadowpane collar at the back, red sateen faux pockets, appliquéd thick cotton lace at collar and cuffs. To fit doll about 22". 5" shoulder width. 12" overall length. $300/400

269. Red Curly Wool Double-Breasted Jacket for Bebe Jumeau, Size 6
Of very plush curly textured red wool, the jacket-sweater features faux-double-breasted front with two rows of brass buttons, white curly wool collar and cuffs of 1/2 length sleeves. Cloth label "6" at in the inside back indicates sizing for Bebe Jumeau, size 6. 5" shoulder width. 20" overall length. $200/250

270. Red Textured Woolen Jacket
Of richly textured wool giving an illusion of thickness, yet being a proper weight for doll wear, the red jacket features shaped front opening with ivory silk sewn-down collar, and 3/4 sleeves with ivory silk sewn-down cuffs. There is self banding at the shoulders and back seams, the jacket is lined in ivory silk, and the collar and cuffs are decorated with thick coral soutache. To fit doll about 22". 6" shoulder width. 12" overall length. $200/300

271. Burgundy Velvet Jacket with Matching Beret
Of very luxurious burgundy velvet in faux double-breasted style with two rows of pearl buttons, rounded collar, coat sleeves with turn-up cuffs, very thickly quilted rose silk lining, the jacket features slightly shaped sides with back flap. With matching beret whose top is of burgundy velvet and whose underbrim and band is of ivory silk faille, ivory sateen lining and silk pom-pom. To fit doll about 28". 9" shoulder width. 12" overall length. 5" inside head width. 8" overall width of cap. $500/700

272. Textured Maroon Velvet Coat with Shaped Collar
Of richly textured maroon velvet, the coat features a fitted bodice above box-pleated front and back, very full 3/4 sleeves with fitted cuffs, fitted neckline with very large diamond-point shaped collar, rose silk lining, hook-and-eye closure at throat. 24". 7" shoulder width. 15" overall length. $400/500

273. Taupe Cashmere Wool and Brown Velvet Coat
Of softest cashmere wool in soft brown taupe, the coat features overcast stitching at the edges, high collar for warmth with very wide shoulder collar of brown velvet with scalloped shaped

taupe edging, long sleeves with pleats at the shoulders for fullness and overcast stitching at cuffs. The collar extends completely around the back. To fit doll about 18". 4 1/2" shoulder width. 11" overall length. 150/200

274. Brown Woolen Coat with Double Collar and Velvet-Lined Straw Bonnet

Of textured brown wool, the coat features fitted yoke above full-length pleats sewn-down for shaping to the waist, very full sleeves with gathers at the shoulders, very wide fitted cuffs, two wide box pleats at the back, two graduated size rounded collars with overcast stitching, pale green silk lining. With tri-color straw bonnet banded by pale brown velvet ribbon, whose underbrim is lined with rich dark brown velvet, ivory silk lining. To fit doll about 20". 5" shoulder width. 14" overall length. 3" inside cap width. 6" overall cap width. $400/500

275. Light Brown Woolen Coat-Dress and Silk Plush Bonnet for Bebe Jumeau, Size 8

Of very luxurious light brown soft wool, the coat-dress features fitted bodice and waist, above a gathered skirt, the bodice overlaid by waist-length cape that achieves its shape by ruching at the collar, band collar, very full gathered 3/4 sleeves with shaped cuffs, hook-and-eye closure. The coat is trimmed with pale coral featherstitching and a silk rosette and streamers at the front waist. Along with wire-framed silk plush bonnet with net stiffening, organza and rose silk ribbons (bonnet trim frail). The coat has original size label "8" inside the collar. 5" shoulder width. 12" overall length. $500/700

276. Cream Mohair Coat with Aqua Wool Trim for Bebe Jumeau, Size 8
Of silk like long mohair plush, the faux-double-breasted coat features two rows of pearl buttons at the front, pale aqua cashmere wool collar and turn-up cuffs with cream soutache trim, ivory sateen lining. The coat has original size "8" inside the collar. 6" shoulder width. 12" overall length. $400/500

277. Cream Mohair Coat with Cream Wool Trim
Of silk like long mohair plush, the coat features cream woolen rounded collar with soutache trim, muslin lining, hook-and-eye closure. To fit doll about 18". 6" shoulder width. 12" overall length. $300/400

278. Cream Mohair Coat for Bebe Jumeau, Size 12
Of very luxurious long curly mohair with silk like finish, the coat features flared sides, 3/4 sleeves, white woolen rounded collar with four bands of cream soutache trim, and cream sateen lining. The coat has original size label "12" inside the collar. 8" shoulder width. 17" overall length. $400/500

279. Waffle-Patterned Jacket with Cap and Muff
Of intricately woven waffle pattern in cream color with interwoven rose design, the flared side coat features white fur collar, long sleeves with white fur cuffs, hook-and-eye closure. With matching fur-edged cap having rose silk bows, and white fur muff with rose silk ties and silk lining. To fit doll about 17". 4" shoulder width. 9" overall length. $200/300

280. Woolen Mohair Knit Four Piece Ensemble
Comprising a textured white flannel coat with button and loop closures, long sleeves with unusually long cuffs, silk lining and large rounded collar of long looped curly mohair. Along with matching dress in intricately woven pattern with diamond-edged hemline, high waist, trimmed in aqua silk ribbons, and with looped curly mohair cap and muff, each silk lined and trimmed in aqua silk ribbons. To fit doll about 15". 3 1/2" shoulder width. 10" overall length dress. $600/900

281. White Woolen Jacket in Original Presentation Box
White boiled wooden jacket to achieve textured look, features small rounded collar, 3/4 coat sleeves, and is presented in original store box with lithograph of winter-coated children on the lid. To fit doll about 15". 4" shoulder width. $150/200

282. Tiny Red Woolen Double-Breasted Jacket
The faux-double breasted jacket with shaped lapels, slit sides, 3/4 length sleeves, white overcast stitching, four tiny brass buttons. To fit doll about 7". 1 1/2" shoulder width.

283. Black Woolen Suit for Gentleman with Wooden Shoes
The five-piece ensemble comprises black woolen suit with fully-lined double-breasted jacket, shaped lapels, faux flap pockets; includes button-fly-front trousers; along with red flannel wool double-breasted vest with shaped lapels, six mother-of-pearl and brass buttons, along with matching mother-of-pearl chain and fob; along with tailored white linen shirt with pearl buttons, constructed cuffs. And with black woolen hat with wide brim, rounded top, velvet band; and wooden shoes with carved detail and original paper label inside the soles. To fit doll about 17". 7" shoulder width. 4" length shoe. $600/800

284. Swedish Folklore Costume with Fur-Trimmed Leather Jacket
Three piece ensemble features white cotton shirt with shaped collar and cuffs, red embroidery detail with black bow-tie; along with yellow sateen short pants with brass-button flap front and red trim and pom-poms. Along with black stockings and long white kid leather coat with fur trim. To fit doll about 14". 4" shoulder width. 9" waist. $300/400

285. Cream Felt Flannel Coat and Cloche with Felt Appliqués
Of thick cream felt flannel, the flared side short coat has double blue felt collars with scalloped edging and colorful polka dot felt appliqués, coat sleeves with matching cuff trim, double border of cream and blue felt along the front and hem of coat with felt colorful appliqués. With matching cream felt cloche trimmed in blue felt. The coat and cloche are presented in their original gift box with 1930's decorations on the box. To fit toddler-bodied doll about 17". 6" shoulder width. 10" overall length. $400/500

286. Grey Woolen Tweed Three-Piece Ensemble
Comprising grey wool tweed skirt with gored shaping and attached bodice of box-pleated cream flannel, along with matching jacket having long sleeves flared wide at the wrists and a capelet collar edged in silk print. Included is matching beret with blue cotton lining that matches the hidden blue cotton sides of bodice. To fit doll about 24". 5" shoulder width. 8 1/2" skirt length from waist. $300/400

287. Maroon Wool Ensemble for Lady Doll
The two-piece maroon wool ensemble features a long hip-length jacket with slim-fitted waist, generous bodice, rounded capelet collar with rose twill lining, pearl and loop closure, fitted belt waist, long coat sleeves with turned-up cuffs. Along with matching slim-waist gored long skirt. Trimmed with white overcast stitching. To fit lady-bodied doll about 21". 5" shoulder width. 8" waist. $700/900

Chapter VI:
Cotton Dresses, 1880–1930

288. French Bisque Doll in Child's Sewing Arrangement Box with Sewing Machine
An 18" bisque socket head doll with blue glass eyes, open mouth, composition body, is presented in her original box along with a toy sewing machine, various fabrics and supplies tied to the box with original blue silk ribbons, threads, bone sewing tools, scissors. The doll wears her original muslin chemise labeled "Bebe Mignon". The set was designed with the idea of a child created a trousseau for the doll, and is preserved in its original state, here unplayed with. 17" x 20" box. $1100/1600

289. French Sewing Machine in Original Box

Cast iron toy sewing machine with gold stenciled designs and working needle, is preserved in its original box with colorful engraving on the lid featuring children sewing costumes for their dolls; two dolls are shown in the image. Along with original instruction sheet for use noting that the machine is a Singer model, and that it can be used on wool, silk, cotton or toile. 6"h. $400/500

290. Large Blue/White Checkered Pinafore Dress

Of crisp blue and white checkered pattern, the open-back cotton dress features high rounded yoke edged with scalloped edge self-ruffle trimmed with white embroidery, full gathered skirt, long full sleeves with set-in buttoned cuffs, two pockets with scalloped-edge embroidered flaps, attached waist tie. To fit doll about 35". 10" shoulder width. $300/400

291. White Cotton Dress with Printed Blue Flowers

Of white cotton printed with vertical bands of abstract blue flowers and stripes, the high-waisted dress features a fitted yoke edged with wide ruffled Bertha collar, very full gathered skirt with additional self-ruffle at the hem, insert drawstring at the hips to give blouson shape, very full 3/4 sleeves with constructed cuff trimmed with ruffle. There is insert and edging lace at yoke, neckline, collar and sleeves. To fit doll about 30". 8" shoulder width. 19" overall length. $300/400

292. Blue/White Checkered Two-Piece Dress
Of tiny blue and white checkered cotton, the ensemble features jacket with very tight ruching at the shoulders opening into gathered front, and ruching at center back, open front with four white buttons and handmade button holes; long sleeves, delicate cutwork borders and featherstitching at neckline, cuffs and hem of blouse. Along with matching skirt having sewn-down pleats to hips and constructed waist. To fit doll about 20". 4 1/2" shoulder width. 10" waist. $200/300

293. Blue Cotton Plaid Pinafore Dress with Embroidered Bib
Of blue plaid cotton, the dress features a very high yoke with square cut neckline above full gathered skirt, full sleeves with fitted cuffs, open back with button and loop at top. With white pique bib outlined and embroidered in dark blue threads, and with gilt brooch. To fit doll about 12". 2 1/2" shoulder width. 8" overall length. $150/250.

294. White Cotton Dress with "Children in the Garden" Fabric Design
Of white textured cotton printed with navy blue designs featuring children in outdoor scenes (playing with dolls, sand pails, gardening) the dress features gathered high-waisted bodice with low rounded neckline, lace Bertha collar, full sleeves with gathered shoulders and wide lace edging, cartridge pleated very full skirt. There is navy blue featherstitching at neckline, sleeves and hem; white buttons with handmade buttonholes. To fit doll about 17". 4" shoulder width. 10" waist. 12" overall length. $200/300

295. Pale Blue Cotton Print High-Waisted Dress
Of pale blue cotton printed with abstract design in white and navy blue, the dress features a high-waist with fitted yoke decorated with simple bretelles and featherstitched white banding, attached sash with double rosettes, full sleeves with wide ruffled bands trim with cotton lace, box-pleated skirt, white button and handmade buttonholes. To fit doll about 15". 3 1/2" shoulder width. 10" overall length. $150/200

296. Blue Polka Dot Dress with Attached Blouse
Of vibrant blue cotton with printed polka dots, the dress features embroidered scalloped edge trim at hem and bodice, dropped waist, attached faux-underblouse with tucked bodice, very full sleeves, lace and cutwork trim at collar and cuffs. To fit doll about 19". 5" shoulder width. 12" overall length. $250/300

297. Navy Blue Cotton Dress
Of crisp navy blue cotton printed with abstract design in red and cream, the dress features sewn-down box-pleated on front and back bodice above set-in waist, full box-pleated skirt, button closure with hidden handmade buttonholes, slightly full sleeves, lace edging at neckline and sleeves, rose silk sash. To fit doll about 18". 4" shoulder width. 10" waist. 12" overall length. $200/250

298. Patterned Cotton Lawn Summer Dress
Of delicate white fabric printed with tiny shaded blue flowers, the dress features a gathered bodice below fitted round neck edged with lace, set-in waistband above gathered skirt with two added wide ruffles of same-fabric, very full sleeves with constructed shape, ruffles at the shoulders, and ruffled edging with lace trim. The dress is completely lined with additional lace-edged dust ruffle and has button and loop closure. To fit doll about 18". 5" shoulder width. 12" waist. 11" overall length. $200/300

299. Navy Blue Polka Dot Cotton Dress
Of navy blue cotton, the dress features slightly dropped waist above shaped bodice trimmed with vertical bands of embroidered cutwork at front and back and lace-trimmed rounded collar; the very full skirt is overlaid with 3/4 length gathered skirt of same fabric and both skirt lengths are trimmed with embroidered cutwork. The dress has full length sleeves with cutwork-edged faux cuffs, and four pearl buttons and buttonholes at the back. To fit doll about 22". 6" shoulder width. 15" overall length. $300/400

300. Fine Muslin Dress with Large V-Shaped Collar
Of natural tightly woven crisp muslin, the dress features a slightly high-waist dress, with sewn vertical tucks at the bodice front overlaid by a large V-shaped collar that extends from the rounded neck band to below the waist, constructed waist above full gathered skirt with center vertical tucks, long sleeves with elbow-length seams for shaping, hook-and-eye closure, cream silk floral embroidery, embroidered cotton band and cotton lace at collar and cuffs. To fit doll about 28". 7 1/2" shoulder width. 20" overall length. $300/400

301. Cream and Blue Textured Cotton Blouson Dress
Of unusual cream fabric with intricate openwork weave and interwoven tiny blue design, the dress features a square-shaped inset yoke above a blouson bodice that achieves its shape from pleats at the yoke border, the set-in waist band, and a support band hidden at the inside. The dress has full-length sleeves and attached belt. There is rich organza trim at the yoke, cuffs and forming two ruffles at the hem, each with embroidered scalloped edging. To fit doll about 24". 6" shoulder width. 14" waist. 19" overall length. $300/400

302. Small Blue and White Pin-Check Cotton Dress
Of very crisp cotton in tiniest blue and white pin-check, the open-back dress with tapered sides features a rounded neckline with banded collar, front and back box pleats sewn-down to the waist, long sleeves with constructed cuffs, two pockets, hemline ruffle, attached waist ties, two buttons and handmade buttonholes at the back. The dress is trimmed with tiny white featherstitching at sewn-down pleats, cuffs, pockets, hemline. To fit doll about 9". 2" shoulder width. 6" overall length. $300/400

303. Tiny Blue and White Flannel Dress
Of tiny navy blue and white checker design, the dropped waist dress has inset cotton lace collar, short sleevelets and scalloped-edge trim at the bottom hem. The dress is trimmed with ice blue silk ribbons, and has muslin lining in skirt to give shape, and tiny hook-and-eye closure. To fit doll about 6". 1 1/2" shoulders. 4" overall length. $200/250

304. Navy Blue Cotton Sateen Dress with Gold Leaf Pattern
Of lustrous navy blue cotton sateen printed with abstract gold leaves and thistles, the dropped waist dress features a rounded collar with high yoke offset by box-pleated ruffle with embroidered diamond-shaped edging, gathered bodice to hips, gathered skirt, very full long gathered sleeves with 3" wide constructed cuffs having four button closures. The bodice is fully lined for shaping, and has two gold buttons and loops at top back, and hook-and-eye hidden closures to hips. To fit doll about 25". 6" shoulder width. 16" overall length. $400/500

305. Blue Chambray Dress with Handmade Rick-Rack
Of crisp blue chambray, the loosely fitted dress features rounded neckline with ruffled self-collar, long sleeves with turned-up cuffs, two rounded pockets, gathered ruffle at the hemline, and attached sash at the back. There is handmade white rick-rack trim at the collar, cuffs, pockets, hem and sash, and six white pearl buttons with handmade buttonholes. To fit doll about 24". 7 1/2" shoulder width. 15" overall length. $300/400

306. Pale Blue Cotton Dress with Cotton Lace Yoke
Of cotton muslin, the dress features bodice with narrow tucking centering a cotton lace yoke, and accented with bands of rose and cream silk ribbons. There are 3/4 length gathered sleeves with ribbons banding and constructed cuffs, banded neckline with lace edging, widely pleated skirt overlaid all around with a ribbon-edged panel that forms a V at the front of the skirt, two button closure with handmade buttonholes. To fit doll about 19". 5" shoulder width. 14" waist. 15" overall length. $200/300

307. Pale Blue Chambray Pinafore over White Cotton Dress
A crisp white cotton dress with high fitted yoke above full gathers, gathered long sleeves with set-in cuffs, rounded neckline with cutwork ruffled collar, button closures at cuffs and back of collar, is topped by a blue cotton chambray sleeveless open-back pinafore with cutwork edging at neckline and white featherstitching, blue silk bows at shoulders. To fit doll about 16". 4 1/2" shoulder width. 10" overall length. $300/400

308. Blue Cotton Chambray Dress with Pockets
Of crisp blue chambray with flared sides and rounded collar, the dress features long coat sleeves with constructed button cuffs, two rounded pockets, attached button sash at the back, four pearl buttons and handmade buttonholes, and is trimmed with double bands of white cotton edging at neckline, cuffs, pockets, hem, sash, and down the entire back. To fit doll about 21". 6" shoulder width. 14" overall length. $300/400

309. Commercial Cotton Dress with Coat
Sleeveless dropped waist cotton dress with cotton lace edging at neckline, along with pale blue crisp batiste coat with interwoven white vertical threads, V-shaped black silk collar with wide band of lace edging, gold decorative buttons. To fit doll about 14". 3" shoulder width. 9" overall length. $100/200

310. Blue Commercial Cotton Dress with Very Wide Bertha Collar
Of crisply started textured blue cotton with short sleeves, white blouson bodice, set-in waist, gathered skirt with band of wide hem band, 3" wide ruffled lace Bertha collar with blue silk bows, along with blue knit stockings. To fit doll about 13". 2 1/2" shoulder width. 8" loose waist. 8" overall length. $150/200

311. Red Cotton Commercial Dress
Of crisp red cotton sateen the dropped waist dress features cream openwork bodice overlaid by very wide red bretelles trimmed with a wide band of lace, cream and black braid, red silk ribbon with red silk rosette. With short sleeves, lace hip sash, and pleated skirt with net lining. To fit doll about 15". 4" shoulder width. 10" overall length. $200/300

312. Blue Cotton Commercial Dress with Red Shoes and Stockings
Of pale blue cotton chambray, the dress features a fitted yoke above box-pleated skirt, short full sleeves, detachable Bertha collar. The dress and collar are trimmed with white cotton lace and red embroidered blue ribbon banding. Along with red leatherette shoes with silver buckles and red cotton stockings. To fit doll about 10". 2 1/2" shoulder width. 6 1/2" overall length. 1 3/4" shoe length. $300/400

313. Tiny Blue/White Checkered Dress with Muslin Apron
Of blue and white checkered pattern, the simple dress with rounded neckline and short sleeves, each edged with lace, has muslin apron with pleated bodice, lace waist, long ties, and a wide colorful border depicting a parade of Dutch children. To fit doll about 8". 2" shoulder width. 5" overall length. $100/200

314. Blue and White Striped Cotton Dress with Muslin Bodice and Cuffs
Of crisp blue and white striped cotton, the dress features gathered bodice and skirt with constructed waist, full-length sleeves with fitted muslin cuffs, self-banded collar, muslin pinafore top that is sewn onto the bodice at the waist. With pearl buttons and handmade buttonholes at back of dress and muslin top. The muslin top and cuffs are decorated with

red banding and soutache embroidery, and there is a row of red embroidery at the hem. Few stains on skirt. To fit doll about 28". 7" shoulders. 14" waist. 20" overall length. $400/500

315. Blue Cotton Chambray Dress with Red Scalloped Edging
Of blue chambray the dropped-waist dress features a square-cut neckline edged with red embroidered scalloping, box pleats that extend down the entire front and back, and at the front are offset by a stitched-down hip sash that loosely buttons at the back. There are full-length gathered sleeves, and red scalloped edging at cuffs and hem. To fit doll about 25". 7 1/2" shoulder width. 17" overall length. $300/400

316. Blue and White Checkered Pinafore Dress
Of blue and white shadowpane checkered pattern, the open-back pinafore dress features slightly dropped waist with inset of V-shaped box pleats above the constructed waistband at front and back, low rounded neckline with pleated self collar, 3/4 full sleeves with constructed cuffs and two button and loop closure, gathered skirt with pockets having pleated bands, red hankie, button and loop closure at the back. To fit doll about 22". 7" shoulder width. 14" waist. 11" overall length. $200/300

317. Red Cotton Dress and Apron with "Children's Parade" Borders
Of red cotton, the dress features fitted bodice with rounded neckline, wide gathered collar of border fabric featuring children in party costumes marching as though in a parade, full gathered skirt with similar border at hemline, full sleeves with constructed cuffs, hook-and-eye closure. There is a separate apron with small bib top, set-in waist with long ties, and patterned design forming the bib, two pockets and wide band at the hem. To fit doll about 22". 6" shoulder width. 14" waist. 15" overall length. $300/400

318. Red Cotton Dress with Cutwork and White Embroidery
Of red cotton made with cutwork and white embroidery oval, having fitted bodice centered by inset panel edged by diamond point ruffles, rounded neckline with ruffled collar, set-in waistband, full gathered skirt with scalloped edging, long sleeves with ruffled scalloped edge cuffs, hook-and-eye closure. To fit doll about 24". 7" shoulder width. 16" waist. 15" overall length. $300/400

319. Red Cotton Chambray Dress with Straw Hat
Of pale-red cotton chambray, the dress features slightly dropped waist with borders of heavy white cotton lace centering a gathered bodice with ruching at the rounded neckline, constructed waistband, long sleeves with gathering at the shoulders and dart-shaping at the wrists, full gathered skirt. Along with wide-brimmed, two-color woven straw hat with red cotton sateen band and streamers. To fit doll about 28". 8" shoulder width. 18" overall length. $300/400

320. Flowered Cotton Dress with Shirring
Of cream cotton with delicately printed flowers, the loosely fitting dress features center panel at both front and back with shirring at top and bottom to create gathered effect, low-rounded collar with scalloped trim border, short sleeves with box pleats, defined hip border with two ruffled borders below. The dress is decorated with embroidered red floral edging at collar, sleeves and skirt ruffles. To fit doll about 15". 5" shoulder width. 10" overall length. $300/400

321. Red Leather Shoes with Triple Ankle Straps
Of red leather with cream stitching, the shoes features three sets of ankle straps. There are leather bows, silver buckles and buttons on each strap and the shoe front, tan leather undersoles. 3"l. $300/400

322. Red Cotton Dress with Dropped Waist
Of red cotton with V-shaped tucks centering a center panel of gathers, bretelles, rounded collar with box-pleated cotton and lace collars, full sleeves with dart-shaped snug lower sleeves, lace-edged sleeve bands, full gathered skirt with ruffled overlay, red silk shoulder bows. To fit doll about 17". 4" shoulder width. 12" overall length. $300/400

323. Red/Cream Checkered Dress with Velvet Trim and Muff
Of heavy textured cotton in a tiny red and cream shadow-check design, the dress features a dropped waist with box pleats at front and back bodice, centered cartridge pleats at hip seam, elbow-length sleeves. The dress is decorated with red velvet yoke, sleeve bands and detachable hip sash. There is red feather-stitching at yoke and sleeves. The dress is fully lined with pearl button at back. Along with red woolen muff with muslin lining and red silk straps. To fit doll about 18". 4" shoulder width. 12" overall length. $400/500

324. Red/Brown Cotton Plaid Dress with Redwork Embroidery
Of cotton plaid, the fabric cut in an unusual manner to create a diagonal effect, the dress features a V-shaped pleated bodice edged by bretelles of graduated width red-embroidered trim, fitted bodice, full sleeves with red-embroidered shaped cuffs, full gathered skirt with ruching detail at waist. The skirt bottom is bordered by scalloped-edge red-embroidered border, seven pearl buttons and buttonholes at the back. To fit doll about 18". 4" shoulder width. 12" loose waist. 11" overall. $300/400

325. Three-Piece Cotton Print Costume
Each of printed homespun-like cotton with stenciled designs, comprising shirt top with embroidery at hemline; flower-print petticoat with ruffled border and drawstring waist; and red polka dot skirt with fanciful border design of clowns and circus performers, with constructed waist band. To fit doll about 18". 4" shoulder width. 7" waist. $400/500

326. Rose Cotton Sateen Dress with Bonnet and Shoes
Of polished rose cotton sateen with woven flecks, the dress features box-pleats at V-shaped yoke, self-banded collar, dropped waist with blouson bodice, gathered skirt with flared side, full sleeves with sewn-down pleats and constructed cuffs, self sash, six narrow decorative tucks on skirt, with lace trim, hook-and-eye closure. Along with woven rose bonnet trimmed with silk flowers and lace. Includes ivory silk shoes with rose cotton lining, rose pom-pom, white soles. To fit doll about 23". 5" shoulder width. 14" overall length. $800/1000

327. Pink Muslin Factory Dress
Of pink loosely woven muslin and constructed in very simplistic manner, the dropped waist dress has narrow-pleated skirt with lace trim, blouson-bodice with lace yoke and flower-printed muslin collar with lace-edging. To fit doll about 14". 3" shoulder width. $100/150

328. Tiny Pink Cotton Dress
Of printed pink cotton with striped design, the dress features a slightly dropped waist with ruching above the waist band, rounded neckline with lace edging, elbow-length sleeves with lace edging, full gathered skirt, pearl buttons with loop closure. To fit doll about 8". 2" shoulder width. $100/150

329. Pale Yellow and Rose Dress with Undergarments and Parasol
Of textured pale yellow cotton, the loosely-gathered dress features a fitted yoke of rose cotton overlaid with lace and edged by rose silk ribbons and a very wide lace Bertha collar that extends completely around the back of the dress and over the shoulders of the very full lace-edged sleeves. There are two rows of tucks around the skirt. Along with two cotton undergarments, and a wooden-handled parasol with rose sateen cover. To fit doll about 25". 5" shoulder width. 17" overall length. $500/700

330. White Cotton Pinafore Dress with Bertha Collar in Original Box
Of textured white cotton, the open-backed pinafore dress features square-cut neckline, wide Bertha collar with cutwork and embroidery, full gathered skirt, sleevelets with scalloped edging, tucks around the hem, brass bebe pin, rose silk sash. The doll is presented in its original gift box with lithograph decoration. To fit doll about 17".
4 1/2" shoulder width. 13" overall length. $300/400

331. Rose Straw and Cutwork Bonnet and Ivory Satin Shoes for Bebe Jumeau, Size 11
Constructed of bands of woven rose-tinted straw in alternate patterns, the bonnet is shaped to fit the head, has inlaid cutwork cotton panel and is decorated with puffed silk flower buds. Along with ivory silk shoes with rose silk bows, ankle straps, leather soles marked "11 Paris Depose" and bee stamp. 3 3/4"l. shoes $300/400

332. Pair, Yellow Cotton Dresses for Twins, with Undergarments
Each is of yellow cotton with blouson bodice, full pull sleeves, rounded neckline with lace collar, gathered skirt with three rows of tucking, wide waist sash. Along with two complete sets of five undergarments and black socks for each. To fit doll about 16". 4" shoulder width. 12" overall length. $300/400

333. Cotton Print Dress with Attached Lace Blouse and Straw Bonnet
The dress is designed to appear as a pinafore over lace blouse, but is actually a one-piece dress, with gathered bodice and pleated skirt of textured cream cotton, and blouse of dotted tulle. With lace silk sash and silk ribbons at shoulders. Along with straw bonnet with wide brim turned up at one side, ivory silk ruffle, muslin lining. To fit doll about 14". 3" shoulder width. 8" overall length. $400/500

334. White Cotton Batiste Dress with Straw Bonnet and Watch
Of delicate white cotton, the dropped waist dress features narrow tucks on the bodice overlaid by a very large V-shaped collar, fitted sleeves, two-layered skirt of graduated lengths. The collar, sleeves and both skirt layers are edged by very wide lace borders. There is a blue silk hip sash, gilt brooch pin with attached enamel backed pocket watch and a straw bonnet with blue silk band and bows, muslin lining. To fit doll about 17". 4" shoulder width. 13" overall length. $400/500

335. White Cotton Cutwork Dress with Straw Bonnet
Of fine white cotton and white cotton cutwork, the dress features a rounded neckline with scalloped edge cutwork collar, dropped waist bodice with panels of very narrow tucks alternating with panels of cutwork. The sleevelets, waistband, and very full gathered skirt are of extravagantly worked embroidered cutwork. Along with yellow straw woven bonnet decorated with blue velvet ribbons and yellow and white flowers, cream silk lining. To fit doll about 27". 7" shoulder width. 17" overall length. $500/700

336. Two Cotton Costumes for Little Dolls
Comprising white dotted Swiss dress with high waist, bodice tucks centering a lace panel, tucks at bottom of gathered skirt, full long sleeves, with muslin apron having black stitched outline. And white pique boy's romper suit with black polka dots, pleated collar, button attachment at waist. To fit dolls about 9". $300/400

337. Two Dresses for Bleuette
Comprising navy blue cotton dress with red and white rick-rack trim and buttons, white rounded collar, puff sleeves. And rose tweed cotton dress with shaped waist, pointed collar and cuffs, leatherette belt. From Gautier-Langereau for Bleuette. $300/400

338. French Doll-Sized Mannequin with Red Muslin Cover
The mannequin form with adult female shaping to accommodate fashion of the late 19th century is covered with unusual red sateen, with carved wooden stand, finial and arm hole covers. The wooden stand and front of form have (illegible) maker's name. 31"h. $500/700

339. French Doll-Sized Mannequin with Red Muslin Cover
Nearly identical to #338, with red wooden stand and finial. 30"h. $500/700

340. French Doll-Sized Mannequin with Red Velvet Cover Marked "Buste Girard"
Very shapely mannequin form with red velvet cover, grey painted finial cap and arm hole covers, stamped "Buste Girard Paris" on the base. $700/900